Upgrading
the American Police

CHARLES B. SAUNDERS, JR.

Upgrading the American Police

Education and Training for Better Law Enforcement

THE BROOKINGS INSTITUTION
Washington, D.C.

© 1970 by

THE BROOKINGS INSTITUTION
1775 Massachusetts Avenue, N.W., Washington, D.C. 20036

ISBN 0–8157–7712–4
Library of Congress Catalog Card Number 70–108836

2 3 4 5 6 7 8 9

THE BROOKINGS INSTITUTION is an independent organization devoted to nonpartisan research, education, and publication in economics, government, foreign policy, and the social sciences generally. Its principal purposes are to aid in the development of sound public policies and to promote public understanding of issues of national importance.

The Institution was founded on December 8, 1927, to merge the activities of the Institute for Government Research, founded in 1916, the Institute of Economics, founded in 1922, and the Robert Brookings Graduate School of Economics and Government, founded in 1924.

The general administration of the Institution is the responsibility of a self-perpetuating Board of Trustees. The trustees are likewise charged with maintaining the independence of the staff and fostering the most favorable conditions for creative research and education. The immediate direction of the policies, program, and staff of the Institution is vested in the President, assisted by an advisory council chosen from the staff of the Institution.

In publishing a study, the Institution presents it as a competent treatment of a subject worthy of public consideration. The interpretations and conclusions in such publications are those of the author or authors and do not purport to represent the views of the other staff members, officers, or trustees of the Brookings Institution.

Foreword

In an era when crime ranks in the forefront of domestic problems and the administration of criminal justice is a major concern of public officials and of the public, policemen responsible for keeping the peace and enforcing the laws are subject to severe pressures and tensions. Whether and how policemen are prepared to meet these pressures and tensions is a question of fundamental importance to the everyday life of most Americans.

Wide variations in standards of police performance mean lack of equal protection of the laws for citizens in different jurisdictions. Is this the inevitable cost of a democratic system's need to maintain local control of the police function? Or can we be decentralized and have excellence in our police too?

How to attract and retain persons with the qualities and skills needed by a modern police force remains a critical question that too few local, state, and federal officials have been willing to face. This reluctance is the more remarkable because, for more than half a century, informed observers have emphasized the crucial relation between the quality and training of police personnel and the effectiveness of law enforcement. Raymond B. Fosdick, one of the founders of the Brookings Institution and author of the first scholarly assessment of the police in America, wrote in 1920 that "the heart of the police problem is one of personnel," and that "the quality of a department's work depends on the observation, knowledge, discretion, courage, and judgment of the men, acting as individuals."

Fosdick's observations have since been affirmed repeatedly by leaders in the law enforcement field. In 1967 the President's Commission on Law Enforcement and Administration of Justice reported serious deficiencies in police personnel and emphasized that "widespread improvements in the strength and caliber of police manpower ... are the basic essentials for achieving more effective and fairer law enforcement." Yet the Omnibus Crime Control and Safe Streets Act of 1968—a landmark recognition of the federal role in strengthening the nation's police forces, enacted after lengthy congressional consideration—did little to improve the qualifications and preparation of police personnel.

This study turns the focus once again on "the heart of the police problem"—the problem of personnel. It summarizes what is known about police deficiencies, examines the qualifications and training necessary for effective performance, considers why these needs have been so long neglected, and suggests the kinds of programs and policies that would enable the federal government to play a responsible role in attacking this critical national manpower problem.

The study was conducted under the guidance of Gilbert Y. Steiner, Director of Brookings' Governmental Studies Program, to whom the author is indebted for encouragement and support. The author wishes to express appreciation to James L. Sundquist of the Brookings staff for helpful suggestions in organizing the final version, and to dozens of police and law enforcement officials who cooperated in its preparation. He is also grateful to Janet Smith and Amelia Suttle, who typed the manuscript; to Nancy C. Romoser, who edited it; and to Helen B. Eisenhart, who prepared the index.

As in all Brookings studies, the views expressed are solely those of the author and should not be attributed to the Brookings Institution, its trustees, officers, or staff.

KERMIT GORDON
President

February 1970
Washington, D.C.

Contents

CHAPTER ONE

A Neglected Element
of Law Enforcement

OF ALL THE DOMESTIC PROBLEMS troubling the American people, crime reached the top of the list in 1968. For the first time in three decades of opinion sampling, the Gallup poll found that citizens ranked crime as the most serious national issue (ahead of civil rights, the cost of living, and poverty) and the most important local issue as well (ahead of schools, transportation, and taxes).[1] Three persons in ten, and four in ten for both women and residents of larger cities, admitted being afraid to go out alone at night in their own neighborhoods.

The pollsters' finding was not really surprising: Federal Bureau of Investigation statistics showed the crime rate rising almost nine times as fast as the population.[2] Nor was it news to any politician in touch with his constituents: in January Congress reacted coolly to the rest of President Lyndon B. Johnson's State of the Union message but roared approval when he denounced "crime in the streets." The Omnibus Crime Control and Safe Streets Act of 1968, a complex and controversial attempt to reduce crime and improve the effectiveness of law enforcement, became law five months later.

1. *New York Times*, Feb. 28, 1968.
2. *Ibid.*, Dec. 12, 1967.

1

Only a few years earlier such legislation would have been unthinkable. The words "crime," "police," and "law enforcement" cannot be found in the subject index of the 1960 presidential campaign speeches of John F. Kennedy and Richard M. Nixon. Nor are they discussed in the report of the President's Commission on National Goals, the Rockefeller Panel Reports, or the Republican party platform of the same year (the lengthy Democratic platform included a cursory mention of rising crime). Not until the 1964 presidential campaign was crime recognized as a national policy issue. The following year Congress passed the Law Enforcement Assistance Act of 1965, a modest grant program which nevertheless expressed a national concern for the adequacy of local police agencies. In the same year, establishment of the presidential Commission on Law Enforcement and Administration of Justice assured further federal involvement.

In 1967, the commission issued a comprehensive report which documented the devastating impact of crime on the national consciousness. It found that crime had "eroded the basic quality of life" for many citizens,[3] and recommended more than two hundred specific proposals for action involving all levels of government and society at large. Emphasizing the magnitude of the task, the commission called for a long, hard, and costly national commitment. There are no simple solutions, it warned, but America can control crime. Broad action must be taken to improve the total system of criminal justice, including the police, the courts, and the correctional system. Better techniques must be developed for dealing with individual offenders; more and better personnel are needed, and they must be given greater technological and research support and greater financial resources. Individual citizens, business and civic groups, schools, and religious institutions, as well as governments, must assume greater responsibilities in the effort to strengthen law enforcement and reduce criminal

3. U.S. President's Commission on Law Enforcement and Administration of Justice, *The Challenge of Crime in a Free Society* (Government Printing Office, 1967), p. v.

opportunities. And at the same time, society must mount a more determined war against poverty and unemployment, discrimination, and the host of social causes of crime.

Directly or indirectly, most of the commission's recommendations dealt with the police, the most visible front line of the criminal justice system. The special problem areas treated in the report—juvenile delinquency, organized crime, narcotics and drug abuse, drunkenness, firearms control, the application of science and technology, the need for research—inevitably concern questions of police organization and operations. A separate chapter and a separate task force report detailed the needs of police agencies, calling for reforms in their traditionally monolithic personnel structure; higher standards of selection and training; more effective community relations; better management, including improved utilization of manpower, clarification of operational policies, and modernization of communications; and greater coordination of services and functions among police forces.

Underlying all its recommendations dealing with the police was a persistent theme: that "widespread improvement in the strength and caliber of police manpower . . . are the basic essentials for achieving more effective and fairer law enforcement." [4] The commission's Task Force on the Police found that "the failure to establish high professional standards for the police service has been a costly one, both for the police and for society. Existing selection requirements and procedures in the majority of departments . . . do not screen out the unfit." [5] Departments throughout the nation maintain a "grossly inadequate" level of training—fragmented, sporadic, and poorly designed to meet the law enforcement needs of a modern urban society.[6] They also face a growing recruitment problem.

4. *Ibid.*, p. 294.
5. U.S. President's Commission on Law Enforcement and Administration of Justice, *Task Force Report: The Police* (Government Printing Office, 1967), p. 125.
6. *Ibid.*, pp. 36–37.

Such criticisms of the police are not new. Almost half a century earlier, the first scholarly inquiry in the field concluded that "the heart of the police problem is one of personnel." [7] Through the years other observers and leaders in law enforcement have agreed, calling urgently for higher standards of police selection and training. Yet there is little indication that this crucial point is understood or accepted by the general public or their elected representatives. The police remain generally undermanned, underqualified, poorly paid, and poorly regarded by their fellow citizens whose laws and lives they are sworn to protect. "The heart of the police problem"—the question of personnel—is generally neglected in public discussions of crime and law enforcement.

No matter what the level of public understanding and support, it would be difficult to upgrade the American police system, which has been described as a "sprawling, complex, expensive, inefficient, and confused pattern of vertical and horizontal duplication, fragmentation, and overlapping." [8] It is really not a system at all, but a collection of 40,000 units without systematic relationship, employing about 400,000 persons. Excluding federal and state enforcement and regulatory officers, whose functions are highly specialized, and state police, whose main function is highway patrol, police service at the local level is the responsibility of no less than 39,750 separate agencies employing 308,000 full-time officers. Fifty-five of these agencies located in the largest cities account for over a third of all personnel; the rest are distributed among 39,695 county or local units—most of them small forces maintained by townships, boroughs, and villages.

America's police agencies, then, are characterized as much by their differences as by their similarities. This fact tends to restrict the citizen's view of police needs and problems. He may be unaware of, and unconcerned with, the situation outside his own

7. Raymond B. Fosdick, *American Police Systems* (The Century Co., 1920), p. 270.
8. Donal E. J. MacNamara, "American Police Administration at Mid-Century," *Public Administration Review*, Vol. 10 (Summer 1950), p. 181.

immediate neighborhood or place of business. Scholarship has added little to popular enlightenment. Social scientists have only begun to do research on the police, and generalizations from their limited data are hazardous because of the remarkable variety of law enforcement agencies.

The nation's press reflects the public concern with isolated symptoms of crime. Articles on police problems usually focus on the technology and weaponry needed to combat riots, organized crime, the drug traffic, juvenile delinquency, and vice or on the special training necessary to improve police-community relations or contain civil disturbances. The quality and the capacities of personnel receiving the equipment and training are rarely investigated.

Throughout the country, a campaign to "Support Your Local Police" has gained some currency, but it is counterfeit. The campaign is a recruiting device of the John Birch Society,[9] and its slogan is an obvious appeal to white backlash sentiment. It has produced a rash of bumper stickers but no grass-roots support for the higher taxes necessary to pay for better qualified, better trained police manpower.

Even so, progress has been made. Decades of effort by the International Association of Chiefs of Police, the FBI, and enlightened leaders in the field have resulted in some improvement. Over thirty states have passed legislation setting minimum standards for selection and training (although in almost half of these states the laws are voluntary and funds for implementing them are insufficient). A growing number of local agencies have taken steps toward greater professionalization (but the goal of professionalism is often confused with a narrow concept of mechanical efficiency). Progress in any event has been sporadic and due more to the persistence of individual spokesmen for reform within the field than to any notable increase in public support for repairing personnel deficiencies.

9. See Benjamin R. Epstein and Arnold Forster, *Report on the John Birch Society* (Vintage, 1966), pp. 51–52.

Despite rising concern with the need for better law enforcement, the public dialogue continues to overlook the manpower problems that so concerned the President's Commission on Law Enforcement. Local officials still find it easier to suggest more men and better equipment than to seek better men and better training. At the national level, police personnel deficiencies have been virtually ignored. In the extensive hearings and debates which led to the omnibus crime bill of 1968, discussion centered on proposals to punish rioters, outlaw the Mafia, overturn Supreme Court decisions, broaden the use of wiretapping, and provide funds for more weaponry and equipment. Of more than four hundred "anticrime" measures introduced in the Ninetieth Congress, only two dealt directly with the need to upgrade police personnel, and no hearings were held on either of them.

Although the President's Commission on Law Enforcement found that improvement of local law enforcement must necessarily involve long-range federal programs to raise the standards of police education and training, the Omnibus Crime Control Act contains relatively little assistance for these areas. Funds under the act may purchase more equipment and facilities and specialized training for some personnel in selected departments, but this will hardly assure better and more extensive training at all levels of the career structure in police agencies throughout the country. Limited funds allocated to encourage enrollment in college-level law enforcement programs will not begin to attract qualified young men into police careers in the numbers needed. Nor does the legislation provide incentives to upgrade standards of police selection and performance, despite evidence presented by the commission that wide disparities exist in the quality of law enforcement within regions, states, and even single communities.

Exactly how these omissions weaken the legislation is difficult to assess. The value of higher education for law enforcement cannot be measured precisely, any more than for any other occupation. As an element in the selection process, level of schooling is only a very rough measure of intelligence, which must be tested further and weighed with other factors of character, personality, and background. Likewise, the amount and quality of training cannot assure competent and dedicated personnel. Sound policies for utilization of personnel and efficient organization and management of police departments are also important. Furthermore, while extension of opportunities for education and training of policemen may be the best hope for attracting more qualified persons into the field and improving the individual officer's capacities to perform his duties, most communities are unwilling or unable to provide such opportunities.

Yet citizens in all communities are demanding more effective law enforcement. The call for "law and order" can be heard above the din of protest and violence which has disrupted America's streets and campuses. Inescapably, the police are at the vortex of the social storm sweeping the country, either as scapegoats for larger problems or as representatives of the established order, which is itself under attack. They are in the middle of competing forces, some calling for order and demanding that civil authorities "take the handcuffs off the police," others protesting injustice and seeking reforms of the system, and some of the latter group increasingly defiant of all existing authority. The increasing pressures on law enforcement personnel are evident in the growth of right-wing organizations within their ranks and in other signs of alienation.[10]

If the first responsibility of government in a time of social unrest is to preserve civil peace, the second is to uphold the rule of law without sacrificing it in the name of order. But the first responsibility is challenged by advocates of the doctrine of confrontation, and the second is apparently questioned by a substantial segment of the public. "In our concern over civil disorder, we must not

10. See, for example, the account of right-wing militancy in the New York City department by Sylvan Fox in the *New York Times*, Sept. 6, 1968, and columns by Joseph Kraft, "Two Middle Classes Collide," *Washington Post*, Sept. 1, 1968, and Alan Barth, "Police Sleepiness: Sign of Alienation," *Washington Post*, Dec. 26, 1968.

mistake lawful protest for illegal activities. The guardians of the law are also subject to the law they serve." [11]

The Chicago police riots during the Democratic National Convention of August 1968 dramatized that the right to dissent—one of the nation's founding principles—has become "one of the most serious problems in contemporary democratic society." In full view of television cameras, demonstrators and bystanders alike were subjected to "unrestrained and indiscriminate police violence . . . made all the more shocking by the fact that it was often inflicted upon persons who had broken no law, disobeyed no order, made no threat." [12] The national reaction showed how deeply the "law and order" issue has polarized public opinion. A subsequent Gallup poll found that 56 percent of adults interviewed approved of the way the Chicago police had dealt with the protestors.[13] Responses indicated the extent of public misunderstanding of the police role, crucial though it may be for all citizens. Those who supported the Chicago police action on the grounds that the demonstrators "got what they deserved" did so for the wrong reasons, for in the American system of justice the police have no license to administer punishment at will, regardless of provocation. At the other extreme, many who disapproved indicated just as serious a misunderstanding in their tendency to condemn all police ("pigs") and the entire law enforcement system.

The Chicago incident illustrates the dangers which inadequate enforcement of the laws poses for society. It suggests how readily demands to get tough may be interpreted "by every heavy-handed policeman in the country as a license to beat somebody up— probably somebody poor, black, or young, preferably all three." [14] At the same time, it underlines how difficult the task of preserving

11. *Report of the National Advisory Commission on Civil Disorders* (Government Printing Office, 1968), p. 171.
12. *Rights in Conflict: The Walker Report to the National Commission on the Causes and Prevention of Violence* (Bantam Books, Inc., 1968), pp. xv, 1. Another police riot occurred in New York City shortly thereafter, with the beating of black militants by off-duty policemen (see *New York Times*, Sept. 5, 1968).
13. *New York Times*, Sept. 18, 1968.
14. Tom Wicker, *New York Times*, Oct. 15, 1968.

civil peace becomes when sufficient numbers of the population insist on confrontation as a political technique. That such law enforcement problems have become a nationwide concern is abundantly evident.

Just as real a national concern is the capacity of the police to meet their responsibilities for fighting crime. In this mobile society, police performance in one locality obviously affects law enforcement elsewhere. The crime rate is rising in the suburbs and rural areas as well as in the cities. Recognition that crime is a national problem means, if anything, that coordinated efforts are required at all levels of government. Each of the 39,750 local police agencies contributes to the total effectiveness of law enforcement in the United States—but the quality of each depends primarily on the vagaries of local leadership and citizen concern.

The President's Commission on Law Enforcement estimated that "several hundred million dollars annually could be profitably spent over the next decade" for federal assistance to strengthen the criminal justice system in all its aspects.[15] The commission's rough estimate plainly shows that the $29 million expended for the first full year of the 1968 Omnibus Crime Control Act is only a small first step. Significantly increased expenditures for subsequent years are practically assured. But the fact remains that this landmark national effort to improve local law enforcement fails to recognize "the critical importance of improved education and training in making the agencies of criminal justice fairer and more effective. . . ."[16]

The question must be asked: Why? Why have police manpower needs, which the President's Commission painstakingly and pointedly identified as basic elements of any attempt to improve law enforcement, been overlooked in the developing national effort?

15. U.S. President's Commission on Law Enforcement and Administration of Justice, *The Challenge of Crime in a Free Society*, p. 284.
16. *Ibid.*, p. 285.

It may be argued that the commission's recommendations for federal action in this field lacked specificity. Its report emphasized the nature and extent of police manpower problems but did not consider whether they could be solved or what the likely effect on law enforcement might be. While urging substantial federal assistance for police education and training, the report did not provide clear guidelines for action. It merely suggested some of the types of programs that might be supported, without analyzing which would be most desirable and offer the greatest chance for improvement of police manpower. It failed to explore the appropriate scope, dimensions, and costs of a realistic federal effort. Perhaps this made it easier for Congress to ignore the commission's recommendations for upgrading police manpower; at any rate they were scarcely considered in the development of the Omnibus Crime Control and Safe Streets Act of 1968.

The question remains: Why have the commission's troubling findings about the personnel deficiencies of the nation's police forces been so generally ignored at all levels of government and by the public at large? Was the commission's emphasis on personnel problems justified? If so, what can be done to correct these problems? Can effective corrective programs be instituted on the basis of what is now known about police education and training? What can be said to constitute adequate education and training for police? What can better education and training be expected to accomplish in terms of better law enforcement? If large-scale federal assistance is to be directed to this objective, what forms should it take?

These questions cannot be answered authoritatively. Nevertheless they deserve to be faced, not ignored, as the nation seeks to cope with its mounting problems of crime and violence amid increasing concern for law and order. This study, therefore, attempts to focus attention on the public policy issues raised by the recommendations of the President's Commission for upgrading police personnel. It first summarizes what is known about education and training for law enforcement in order to assess the full implications of the commission's recommendations and explore the dimensions of an effective national program to carry them out.

The limitations of such a study should be apparent. Other aspects of police manpower problems, such as the need for more efficient organization and better utilization of manpower and technology, are beyond its scope. Such factors are, of course, critically important in any effort to improve law enforcement. Unlike the needs for education and training, however, they are receiving increasing attention from within the police service and from scholars and specialists. Nor is any attempt made here to investigate the serious manpower deficiencies in the other sectors of the criminal justice system, the courts and correctional institutions and programs. For an extensive treatment of the needs of the total system, the reader is referred to the comprehensive reports of the President's Commission on Law Enforcement and its nine task forces.

Likewise, these chapters contain little reference to the achievements of individual departments. To dwell on achievements would only reinforce the public apathy that has so long tolerated serious manpower deficiencies in most local departments. By focusing on those deficiencies, their impact on the quality of law enforcement throughout the nation, and the magnitude of the task of overcoming them, this study aims to challenge apathy.

The role of the policeman is discussed in Chapter 2 as a basis for defining the educational and training requirements of the job. Chapter 3 discusses the problems of police quality and quantity, projects future needs, and shows that these needs have received little consideration as a national manpower problem. Chapters 4 and 5 examine the current state of police education and training and their needs for improvement. Chapter 6 presents the dimensions of a realistic national effort to improve education and training for police and considers the possible costs and benefits in terms of the goal of achieving more equitable and effective protection of the laws for all citizens.

The analysis raises serious questions about the thrust of current national efforts to improve law enforcement. It suggests that the deficiencies of police personnel that the President's Commission identified are too important to be ignored. It affirms the commission's finding that more effective and fairer law enforcement must necessarily be based on comprehensive and long-term programs to raise the standards of selection and training in police agencies throughout the country. At the same time, it suggests that major difficulties stand in the way of implementing the commission's recommendations. The distinction between more education and training and better education and training is too little understood. Existing criteria are inadequate to assure that more substantial federal assistance will produce the desired outcome. The benefits to be obtained for the inevitably larger costs cannot adequately be measured. Nevertheless, the difficulties should be faced. The personnel problems of the police constitute a critical national manpower problem too long neglected.

CHAPTER TWO

The Role of the Police

In a time of rising crime and violence, racial conflict, social unrest, and the politics of protest and confrontation, the police have achieved a new visibility. After decades of public neglect, the vital role of the police in society is demonstrated daily in the nation's press. Concerned citizens, public officials, and national commissions testify to the heavy responsibilities borne by the police and the serious consequences which may result when they are unable to meet those responsibilities.

Public Attitudes toward the Police

Yet the increasing attention paid the police reflects widespread misunderstanding of their role. Many Americans view them as solely responsible for controlling crime. But as the President's Commission on Law Enforcement stressed, crime cannot be understood as a narrow range of behavior by certain types of people: it pervades all strata of society, and its control cannot be accomplished by the police or by the courts and correctional system by themselves.

Another serious cause of misunderstanding is the failure to recognize that law enforcement is an occupation demanding a high order of skills and intelligence. This failure contributes in myriad ways to the problems of the police. It helps explain why there is so little public support for efforts to upgrade police personnel and why policemen throughout the nation are so often poorly prepared to perform their essential tasks. It explains the stereotype of the "dumb cop."

The stereotype is confirmed in the memory of many adults who recall the days when any able-bodied man with the proper political allegiance could find a place on the force. American society is still only a few decades away from the time when immigrants, denied employment in the skilled trades, found the urban police force one of the few open avenues to cultural assimilation; when policing in rural areas was largely a job of chasing stray animals, and when frontier justice asked only that the lawman handle a gun.

One commentator has observed that "the American is not overly impressed by police authority, considering the police officer as a badly paid job holder, not above being 'fixed' by a bribe." [1] A remarkably similar assessment was delivered decades earlier:

> There is little conception of policing as a profession or a science to be matured and developed. It is a job, held, perhaps, by the grace of some mysterious political influence, and conducted in an atmosphere sordid and unhealthy.... Instead of confidence and trust, the attitude of the public toward the police is far more often than not one of cynicism and suspicion. [2]

The assumption that anyone with a strong back and a weak mind can walk a beat is reflected in the relatively low rating of police compared with other professions in national surveys of occupational prestige. Police rank forty-seventh on a list of ninety occupations—below machinists, undertakers, electricians, welfare workers, agricultural agents, and all of the professions. [3] At the same time, polls show a markedly higher rating for federal law enforcement agents. [4] This difference may reflect the fact that the

1. Max Lerner, *America as a Civilization* (Simon and Schuster, 1957), p. 433.
2. Raymond B. Fosdick, *American Police Systems* (The Century Co., 1920), p. 380.
3. Robert W. Hodge, Paul M. Siegel, and Peter H. Rossi, "Occupation Prestige in the United States, 1925–1963," *American Journal of Sociology*, Vol. 70 (November 1964), pp. 290–92.
4. Louis Harris, *Washington Post*, July 3, 1966.

work of federal agents is almost entirely investigative, which appeals to the public fascination with the science of criminal detection.[5] Television drama and the literature of detective fiction illustrate this ambivalence toward policemen, portraying them either as supersleuths or as mental pygmies, constantly outwitted by daring criminals and dashing private eyes.

Another element in popular attitudes is fear of a strong police force—a fear deeply ingrained in the national psychology and a major influence in the historical development of our fragmented police system. Fear and distrust of governmental authority are reinforced by strong cultural values emphasizing individual freedom. The police are the most evident symbol of the limitations imposed on the individual. Their intimate involvement in the lives and problems of citizens increases the ambivalence felt toward them. Police deal with people when they are

> most threatening and most vulnerable, when they are angry, when they are frightened, when they are desperate, when they are drunk, when they are violent, or when they are ashamed. . . . [It] is inevitable that the public is of two minds about the police: most men both welcome official protection and resent official interference.[6]

These factors must be reckoned with in any effort to improve law enforcement. They help explain why one of the oldest and most important functions of municipal government has undergone so little substantial reform.

The Police Task: A Historical Perspective

The view of police work as undemanding is an anachronism dating from the early development of metropolitan forces in the mid-1800s as a force of political appointees paid to serve as watchmen. An early student of police administration wrote,

5. Pointed out by Arthur L. Stinchcombe in "Institutions of Privacy in the Determination of Police Administrative Practice," *American Journal of Sociology*, Vol. 69 (September 1962), p. 159.
6. U.S. President's Commission on Law Enforcement and Administration of Justice, *The Challenge of Crime in a Free Society* (Government Printing Office, 1967), pp. 91–92.

It is certainly not necessary and some have even maintained that it is not desirable that police patrolmen be men of large intellectual ability.... [It is] extremely unlikely that, for the present at least, any considerable number of men who have enjoyed even a secondary education will turn to the police business.... The most important asset of the ideal policeman is unquestionably his physical constitution and condition.[7]

But this view of the police was obsolete by the time it appeared in print. In the same year, August Vollmer, chief of police in Berkeley, California, was applying new principles of organization and professionalism which made him a pioneer of scientific criminal investigation and police administration.

A decade later, the first scholarly assessment of American police emphasized that

The heart of police work is the contact of the individual policeman with the citizen.... The action that is first taken by the policeman of lower rank, operating independently, must, in each case, remain the foundation of the department's action ... the quality of a department's work depends on the observation, knowledge, discretion, courage and judgment of the men, acting as individuals.... Only as the training of the policeman is deliberate and thorough, with emphasis on the social implications and human aspects of his task, can real success in police work be achieved.[8]

A concurrent judgment was expressed by Chief Vollmer, then beginning a single-handed campaign within the police profession to raise personnel standards. In 1916 he founded the first school of criminology at the University of California and advertised in the college newspaper for bright young men to enter law enforcement as a career. Vollmer argued that

the police service has been completely revolutionized in the last few years, and an entirely different type of individual is needed. In addition to higher personal qualifications, there must also be added the professional training in order that the service may not be hampered

7. Leonhard Felix Fuld, *Police Administration* (G. P. Putnam's Sons, 1909), pp. 90–91.
8. Fosdick, *American Police Systems*, p. 306.

and police candidates may be educationally equipped to perform the duties that are now assignable to policemen.[9]

Informed observers outside the law enforcement field agreed. An early specialist in public administration called attention to the growth of heterogeneous urban populations and the attendant problems which "this country has barely begun to approach . . . rationally." The police department, as the direct crime prevention agency, "is concerned with a social problem that is interrelated with all the social and economic conditions in the community. . . . Obviously, the task of combatting crime calls for superior abilities together with training and education." [10] Since effective law enforcement may require the exercise of more power than is actually conferred by law, the authority of police to use personal discretion "should be increased and the character of personnel improved so that this discretion will be wisely exercised." [11]

The International City Managers' Association told its membership in 1931 that "because of the enormity of the task of policing a community it is necessary to emphasize the fact that the best human material in the country is none too good for police service." [12] A joint study by the Los Angeles Police Department and the California State Department of Education in the early 1930s found that a competent patrolman should possess knowledge of one hundred fifty-eight different fields.[13]

Bruce Smith, the foremost scholar of police administration, emphasized the human factor in the law enforcement equation in his landmark study which appeared in 1940:

> The policeman's art, then, consists in applying and enforcing a multitude of laws and ordinances in such degree or proportion and

9. Letter (1932) quoted in Donald E. Clark and Samuel G. Chapman, A Forward Step: Educational Backgrounds for Police (Charles C Thomas, 1966), p. 22.

10. Lent D. Upson, Practice of Municipal Administration (The Century Co., 1926), pp. 324–25.

11. Ibid., p. 321.

12. City Managers' Yearbook, 1931 [International City Managers' Association, Chicago], p. 143.

13. U.S. Department of the Interior, Office of Education, Training for the Police Service, Vocational Division Bulletin No. 197, Trade and Industrial Series No. 56 (1938).

in such manner that the greatest degree of social protection will be secured. The degree of enforcement and the method of application will vary with each neighborhood and community. There are no set rules, nor even general guides to policy, in this regard. Each policeman must, in a sense, determine the standard which is to be set in the area for which he is responsible. Immediate superiors may be able to impress upon him some of the lessons of experience, but for the most part such experience must be his own. . . . Thus he is a policy-forming police administrator in miniature, who operates beyond the scope of the usual devices for popular control. . . .

Hence the task of raising the level of police performance does not hinge upon the use of mechanical aids, as so many suppose. It depends upon sound organization and efficient procedures which are applied to—and by—alert and intelligent servants of the police organism. Since the human factor proves the most difficult to control and may actively resist all change, the process of raising the general level of police service sometimes proves to be a lengthy one. . . .[14]

In the last three decades the human factor has assumed ever greater importance as police agencies have had to cope with the tensions and dislocations resulting from population growth, increasing urbanization, developing technology, the civil rights revolution, changing social norms, and a breakdown of traditional values. Such factors have enormously complicated the law enforcement task, making more critical the need for the "truly exceptional men" Vollmer sought in the 1930s.[15]

Today's local patrolman must be aware of these factors and understand their psychological and sociological implications for his community. He must deal with all of its citizens—rich and poor, young and old, of whatever cultural and ethnic backgrounds —in ways which will maintain their support and confidence. He must be able to provide a variety of services while serving as protector of life, property, and personal liberty. He must be a law

14. Smith, *Police Systems in the United States* (Harper & Bros., 1940), pp. 21–22. The continuing validity of this point is indicated by the use of the identical passage two decades later in the second revised edition (Harper & Row, 1960), pp. 19–20.

15. August Vollmer, *The Police and Modern Society* (University of California Press, 1936), p. 223.

enforcement generalist with a working knowledge of federal, state, county, and municipal law, traffic law, and criminal procedures.

The Police Patrolman: A Job Description

The complex demands of the patrolman's job and the attributes required for successful performance have recently been analyzed by a university research team whose findings, reported as a list of essential behavioral requirements, serve as scientific validation of the point Vollmer made three decades earlier. On the basis of extensive field observation, the scholars concluded that a patrolman must

1) endure long periods of monotony in routine patrol yet react quickly (almost instantaneously) and effectively to problem situations observed on the street or to orders issued by the radio dispatcher (in much the same way that a combat pilot must react to interception or a target opportunity).

2) gain knowledge of his patrol area, not only of its physical characteristics but also of its normal routine of events and the usual behavior patterns of its residents.

3) exhibit initiative, problem-solving capacity, effective judgment, and imagination in coping with the numerous complex situations he is called upon to face, e.g., a family disturbance, a potential suicide, a robbery in progress, an accident, or a disaster. Police officers themselves clearly recognize this requirement and refer to it as "showing street sense."

4) make prompt and effective decisions, sometimes in life and death situations, and be able to size up a situation quickly and take appropriate action.

5) demonstrate mature judgment, as in deciding whether an arrest is warranted by the circumstances or a warning is sufficient, or in facing a situation where the use of force may be needed.

6) demonstrate critical awareness in discerning signs of out-of-the-ordinary conditions or circumstances which indicate trouble or a crime in progress.

7) exhibit a number of complex psychomotor skills, such as driving a vehicle in normal and emergency situations, firing a weapon accurately under extremely varied conditions, maintaining agility,

endurance, and strength, and showing facility in self-defense and apprehension, as in taking a person into custody with a minimum of force.

8) adequately perform the communication and record-keeping functions of the job, including oral reports, preparation of formal case reports, and completion of departmental and court forms.

9) have the facility to act effectively in extremely divergent interpersonal situations. A police officer constantly confronts persons who are acting in violation of the law, ranging from curfew violators to felons. He is constantly confronted by people who are in trouble or who are victims of crimes. Besides his dealings with criminals, he has contact with para-criminals, informers, and people on the border of criminal behavior. (He must also be "alley-wise.") At the same time, he must relate to the people on his beat—businessmen, residents, school officials, visitors, etc. His interpersonal relations must range up and down a continuum defined by friendliness and persuasion on one end and by firmness and force at the other.

10) endure verbal and physical abuse from citizens and offenders (as when placing a person under arrest or facing day-in and day-out race prejudice) while using only necessary force in the performance of his function.

11) exhibit a professional, self-assured presence and a self-confident manner in his conduct when dealing with offenders, the public, and the courts.

12) be capable of restoring equilibrium to social groups, e.g., restoring order in a family fight, in a disagreement between neighbors, or in a clash between rival youth groups.

13) be skillful in questioning suspected offenders, victims, and witnesses of crimes.

14) take charge of situations, e.g., a crime or accident scene, yet not unduly alienate participants or bystanders.

15) be flexible enough to work under loose supervision in most of his day-to-day patrol activities (either alone or as part of a two-man team) and also under the direct supervision of superiors in situations where large numbers of officers are required.

16) tolerate stress in a multitude of forms, such as meeting the violent behavior of a mob, arousing people in a burning building, coping with the pressures of a high-speed chase or a weapon being fired at him, or dealing with a woman bearing a child.

17) exhibit personal courage in the face of dangerous situations which may result in serious injury or death.

18) maintain objectivity while dealing with a host of "special interest" groups, ranging from relatives of offenders to members of the press.

19) maintain a balanced perspective in the face of constant exposure to the worst side of human nature.

20) exhibit a high level of personal integrity and ethical conduct, e.g., refrain from accepting bribes or "favors," provide impartial law enforcement, etc.[16]

These behavioral requirements are basic to the job of a patrolman, regardless of the size and nature of the community in which he works. If competent performance of the law enforcement task is expected, these attributes should characterize every member of the force, from the newest recruit to the oldest veteran. They should be standard equipment for any man in uniform, whether he patrols a sleepy rural street, a congested business district, or a ghetto alley.

Numerous proposals have been made for restructuring the patrolman's job by freeing him from such routine tasks as checking parking meters, directing traffic, delivering summonses, or performing social services. None of these proposals would alter the behavioral requirements outlined above. However his job may be restructured, the patrolman will continue to be the first to respond in any community when citizens call to report a serious traffic accident, a noisy crowd of teenagers on the street, trouble in a bar, a domestic quarrel, a mental patient on the loose, a man unconscious on the sidewalk, prowlers in a building, or a neighbor burning trash. The abilities, skills, and intelligence of the men who answer such calls are of vital concern to every member of the community.

16. Melany E. Baehr, John E. Furcon, and Ernest C. Froemel, "Psychological Assessment of Patrolman Qualifications in Relation to Field Performance," Preliminary Report to Office of Law Enforcement Assistance, Department of Justice (processed, 1968), pp. II-3 to II-5. The project was conducted by the Industrial Relations Center of the University of Chicago under a grant to the Chicago Police Department.

THE PEACEKEEPING FUNCTION

One fundamental but generally neglected aspect of the police role is that of peacekeeping. The enforcement function, which occupies only a small part of the policeman's time, is carefully recorded by reporting procedures. The peacekeeping function, which consumes most of the officer's time and includes all occupational routines not directly related to making arrests, is largely unaccounted for. Police departments literally do not know and cannot explain how individual patrolmen spend most of their time. When asked how they discharge the peacekeeping function, officers say they merely use common sense, although they admit that experience is valuable. Police textbooks and manuals give little attention to peacekeeping, except to suggest that it takes personal wisdom, integrity, and altruism. To the public, this phase of the policeman's duties is a constant cause of misunderstanding:

> ... the citizen will observe that when the patrolman is not handling the citizen's momentary emergency, he is standing on a street corner, walking along the sidewalk, or driving a patrol car—apparently "doing nothing." What he *is* doing, of course, is waiting to be called to cope with someone else's emergency, and if he were not "doing nothing" he would not be immediately available. The citizen, forgetting this, is likely to wonder why he isn't out "looking for the man who stole my car," or whatever.[17]

The importance of the peacekeeping function, and its relevance to the question of preparation and training, is emphasized in a psychiatrist's recent study dealing with the treatment of skid row derelicts by the police. He concludes that peacekeeping requires very real practical skills but that the police themselves are not aware of it:

> Quite to the contrary, the ability to discharge the duties associated with keeping the peace is viewed as a reflection of an innate talent of "getting along with people." Thus, the same demands are

17. James Q. Wilson, *Varieties of Police Behavior: The Management of Law and Order in Eight Communities* (Harvard University Press, 1968), p. 26.

made of barely initiated officers as are made of skilled practitioners. Correspondingly, beginners tend to think that they can do as well as their more knowledgeable peers. . . . The license of discretionary freedom and the expectation of success under conditions of autonomy, without any indication that the work of the successful craftsman is based on an acquired preparedness for the task, is ready-made for failure and malpractice. Moreover, it leads to slipshod practices of patrol that also infect the standards of the careful craftsman.

The uniformed patrol, and especially the foot patrol, has a low preferential value in the division of labor of police work. This is, in part, at least, due to the belief that "anyone could do it." In fact, this belief is thoroughly mistaken. At present, however, the recognition that the practice requires preparation, and the process of obtaining the preparation itself, is left entirely to the practitioner.[18]

This conclusion is highly significant for several reasons. It exposes the inadequacies of any view of the police task which undervalues the peacekeeping function. It points up a major aspect of police performance which is seriously neglected in training. It identifies a need for further research to determine with greater precision the requirements for effective police patrol. And it emphasizes that even routine police work requires a high order of abilities and preparation. The general failure to understand this last point (by the police as well as the public) has surely contributed to our society's unwillingness to accord the police status "either in the European sense . . . as representatives of the State or in the more typically American sense of prestige based on a claim of occupational competence." [19]

Still another failure of public understanding is the widely held fiction that a patrolman's job is not discretionary but is simply the enforcement of the law by catching criminals. This combines

18. Egon Bittner, "The Police on Skid-Row: A Study of Peace Keeping," *American Sociological Review*, Vol. 32 (October 1967), p. 715. The vital point in the preceding paragraph of text, that the police establishment virtually ignores peacekeeping skills, is paraphrased from p. 700.

19. David J. Bordua and Albert J. Reiss, Jr., "Environment and Organization: A Perspective on the Police," in *The Police: Six Sociological Essays*, ed. David J. Bordua (John Wiley & Sons, 1967), p. 51.

several mistaken views: that the crime problem is solely the concern of the police, that their task is mainly one of law enforcement, and that this function requires so little intelligence or imagination that anyone can do it.

This fiction has long been cherished by some apologists for the police who hold that they are "only doing their duty" as well as by civil libertarian critics who maintain that police do not have the capacity to exercise discretion and therefore should not be allowed to do so. But as the skid row study cited above illustrates, discretion is the better part of peacekeeping, which in turn is the bigger part of policing. To deny officers the use of discretion is to misconceive their basic function. The only realistic recourse is to insist that their qualifications and training be sufficient to assure that they exercise discretion well.

No matter how well or how poorly qualified to exercise discretion, the police are forced to do so for a variety of reasons. Many of the laws under which they operate are highly ambiguous, either by intent to permit greater flexibility in enforcement or by accident as a result of the limitations of language or of failure to foresee the day-to-day operating problems encountered in enforcement. In addition, some statutes were never intended to be enforced to the letter, and others are simply obsolete. Limitations on manpower and other resources, and the pressures of community standards, also force the exercise of discretion.[20] Whatever the reason, the policeman must often determine the forms of conduct which are to be subject to the criminal process.

If the extent to which police must exercise discretion is underestimated, this is partly because police themselves usually prefer to project an image of impartial, full enforcement without fear or favor. To admit that they ignore the laws under certain conditions might contribute to a breakdown of respect for all laws, raise the possibility of corruption, and imply that other criteria

20. See Herman Goldstein, "Police Discretion: The Ideal versus the Real," *Public Administration Review*, Vol. 23 (September 1963), pp. 142–43.

for enforcement exist which are difficult to spell out and communicate to members of the force as well as the general public.[21]

No code of conduct could possibly cover all circumstances in which policemen must make instantaneous and irrevocable decisions affecting human life and safety, property rights, and personal liberty. Such awesome responsibility for decision making, indeed, sets the police apart from any other profession—after all, the physician may change his diagnosis, the lawyer his pleading. Decisions affecting human life cannot be made more wisely by reducing them to rote and removing police discretion entirely. Ironically, some proponents of this course describe it as "taking the handcuffs off the police." But without discretion, the police are handcuffed to the limited role of unthinking enforcers, powerless to perform the peacekeeping function which is the most challenging and time-consuming part of their job.

DEVELOPMENT OF RESEARCH ON THE POLICE ROLE

If popular stereotypes about the police have been slow to die, one contributing factor has been an absence of research. Until the last decade the police service has had little capacity for, or interest in, the compilation of basic data about operations and performance. Within the field, leaders who have sought higher standards and personnel reforms have based their case on personal experience and observation rather than on the systematic collection of supporting evidence. J. Edgar Hoover, acting on his own understanding of the need for high competence and constant training, built the Federal Bureau of Investigation from an agency which ranked as "one of the worst law enforcement organizations in the country" [22] in the 1920s into an investigative force with a worldwide reputation for effectiveness. Vollmer and other pioneers at

21. *Ibid.* Goldstein nevertheless argues the desirability of publicly acknowledging the need for exercise of discretion as a means of fostering better understanding of the police task and new thinking about ways to improve the criminal justice system.
22. W. R. Kidd, *Police Interrogation* (Basuino, 1940), p. 11.

the local level, however, have not been able to attract the national following and support necessary to bring about the changes they sought in the nation's police forces.

The International Association of Chiefs of Police, founded in 1893 to advance the police service, has only recently developed a strong research component. In its early years the IACP established the first national fingerprint bureau and pioneered a system of uniform crime reporting, functions which were subsequently assumed by the FBI. In 1935 it created a safety division at Northwestern University to provide field services, research, and education in traffic safety. These programs were broadened further in 1959, when they were moved to Washington, D.C., and reorganized under the late Ray Ashworth. Quinn Tamm, a former assistant director of training and inspection for the FBI, was named director of the division in 1961 and enlarged the managerial consulting service for local departments, conducting surveys upon request. Named executive director of the IACP in 1962, Tamm began to build a research base for a vigorous drive to raise standards and promote reform. A research and development division was established to collect statistical data for analysis by a professional staff of researchers and specialists, as well as a professional standards division to produce a variety of training materials which are now used in thousands of local agencies. The Center for Law Enforcement Research and a revamped monthly journal, *The Police Chief*, became vehicles for dissemination of new ideas and research findings to IACP's more than six thousand members and to scholars and others interested in the field.

Another landmark in the development of research on police problems was provided by the President's Commission on Law Enforcement. Its two-year study was conducted by 19 commissioners and 63 staff members, including lawyers, sociologists, psychologists, systems analysts, and a variety of specialists; in addition, there were 175 consultants and hundreds of advisers from the law enforcement and academic communities. Release in 1967 of the commission's report, together with the reports of its task forces, consultants' papers, and surveys, made available an extensive collection of basic data.

Outside of the law enforcement community, the problems of police manpower and organization have been the domain of virtually a single scholar, Bruce Smith, until the last decade. The scanty and usually hostile attention of other scholars served more to confirm than question the stereotypes of the police. A sociology text of 1939 pictured a police system which "generally operates in a lawless manner and breeds lawlessness," full of graft, collusion, and brutality.[23] A 1943 criminology text still widely used in American colleges states without qualification that "the chief criticisms of the American police, all of a serious nature, are: (1) their subservience to political bosses through a system peculiar to American cities; (2) lack of professional training and ignorance of the law and of the duties inherent in their jobs; and (3) their ruthless 'third degree' methods." [24]

Such blanket condemnations of the police are now being reconsidered and revised. One criminologist has recently advocated a strengthening and broadening of governmental police power as the best defense against the fragmentation of the social structure by militant interest groups: "General recognition and appreciation of the integrative function of the police power to maintain a stable society in stress and emergency and, for [that] matter on an everyday basis in a large, urban, complex society is necessary to achieve orderly living." [25] Another study has emphasized that the "police above all link daily life to central authority; moral consensus is extended through the police as an instrument of legitimate coercion. At the same time the police in performing this function often deflect the hostility of the mass from the class

23. Nathaniel F. Canter, *Crime and Society* (Henry Holt & Co., 1939), p. 72.
24. Harry Elmer Barnes and Negley K. Teeters, *New Horizons in Criminology* (Prentice-Hall, 1943), p. 258.
25. Vernon Fox, "Sociological and Political Aspects of Police Administration," *Sociology and Social Research*, Vol. 51 (October 1966), p. 43.

targets to the police themselves. . . ." [26] Elsewhere its authors have written:

> Although the police are formally organized to enforce the law and maintain public order, it is apparent that they are involved at the same time in enacting justice. It is important to note that all three key terms—order, legality and justice—are ambiguous terms in any social system. But what philosophers, social scientists, and lawyers have argued over for centuries, the police must do every day.[27]

Scholars are thus beginning to give explicit recognition to the extraordinary variety of demands upon the police and their need for a sophisticated arsenal of highly developed interpersonal skills as well as intelligence:

> In the heterogeneous milieu of metropolitan areas, the range and number of values and norms incorporated into vaguely differentiated subcultures present police officers with a variety of offenses against a primarily middle-class legal structure conditioned by the offenders' memberships in these subcultures. Perhaps equally important from the standpoint of police work is that these subcultures also condition the manner in which their members will respond to variations in police handling of citizens. Thus, a police officer whose background is likely to be middle or lower-middle class in nature cannot rely on his common sense or past experiences with the middle-class segments of the community when he attempts to gain voluntary compliance from those whose common sense is predicated on values and norms at variance with his own.[28]

Legal scholars, also, are increasingly accepting the necessity for police to exercise discretion, whereas before their primary concern had been for police transgressions of lawful conduct:

> The policeman's lot is indeed a difficult one. He is charged with applying or enforcing a multitude of laws and ordinances in a degree or proportion and in a manner that maintain a delicate balance

26. David J. Bordua and Albert J. Reiss, Jr., "Law Enforcement," in *The Uses of Sociology*, ed. Paul F. Lazarsfeld, William H. Sewell, and Harold L. Wilensky (Basic Books Inc., 1967), p. 282.

27. Bordua and Reiss, "Environment and Organization: A Perspective on the Police," pp. 32–33.

28. John H. McNamara, "Uncertainties in Police Work: The Relevance of Police Recruits' Backgrounds and Training," in *The Police: Six Sociological Essays*, ed. David J. Bordua, p. 168.

between the liberty of the individual and a high degree of social protection. His task requires a sensitive and wise discretion in deciding whether or not to invoke the criminal process. He must not only know whether certain behavior violates the law but also whether there is probable cause to believe that the law has been violated. He must enforce the law, yet he must also determine whether a particular violation should be handled by warning or arrest. . . . He is not expected to arrest every violator. Some laws were never intended by the enactors to be enforced, and others condemn behavior that is not contrary to significant moral values. If he arrested all violators, the courts would find it impossible to do their work, and he would be in court so frequently that he could not perform his other professional duties. Consequently, the policeman must judge and informally settle more cases than he takes to court.[29]

The new and sympathetic interest in the police role has also stimulated research in the improvement of police selection standards and techniques by psychologists and psychiatrists. One study, noting that "the increasing complexity of urban law enforcement has placed a premium upon choice of properly qualified men who, by reason of intelligence, temperament, and training, can adequately meet the challenge of social conditions in our metropolitan cities," suggests that personality characteristics provide an index of effective police performance.[30] Emotional stability is listed as most crucial, since it "implies resilience and good judgment in the face of unpredictable surprises and pressures of urban police work." Other factors include social motivation; freedom from crippling personal pathology such as sadism, paranoia, or other forms of emotional illness; freedom from crippling social pathology such as excessively authoritarian attitudes, racial prejudice, or extremist social views; a high level of energy and self-assertion; effective intelligence under conditions of stress; and a

29. Richard C. Donnelly, "Police Authority and Practices," *Annals of the American Academy of Political and Social Science*, Vol. 339 (January 1962), pp. 91–92.

30. Robert B. Mills, Robert J. McDevitt, and Sandra Tonkin, "Selection of Metropolitan Police Officers," paper presented at a convention of the American Psychological Association, Los Angeles, Sept. 6, 1964.

facility for written and spoken expression of an order not necessarily guaranteed by a high school diploma or even college credits.

Another more extensive study has concluded that the most desirable attributes for successful patrolmen "are all related to stability—stability in the parental and personal family situations, stability stemming from personal self-confidence and the control of emotional impulses, stability in the maintenance of cooperative rather than hostile or competitive attitudes, and stability deriving from a realistic rather than a subjective orientation toward life." [31] The authors stress that their results "are in direct contradiction to . . . those who maintain that psychopathic or even pathological characteristics are required for patrolmen success, i.e., that you have to 'set a thief to catch a thief.' "

The growing body of scholarship is also beginning to influence personnel specialists, who after decades of using identical qualifications and salary scales to recruit both police and firemen, are now advocating separate pay scales:

> The fact is that the cop on the beat must be better qualified to cope with more different and difficult things in more independent manner than the entrance level firefighter. This fact has not yet been adequately recognized in the establishment of minimum qualification requirements.[32]

The scholarly reassessment of the police role and its requirements now under way provides a hopeful basis for improved understanding and support of higher selection and training standards in the future. But the problem is not simply one of awakening the public and its elected officials to the need for higher standards for the police. The police themselves must accept a view of professionalism which goes beyond the improvement of technical skills and managerial efficiency to a broader understanding of the role of law enforcement in democratic society.

---

31. Baehr, Furcon, Froemel, "Psychological Assessment of Patrolman Qualifications in Relation to Field Performance," p. IX-9.
32. Carl F. Lutz, *Relating Police and Fire Department Salaries* (Public Personnel Association [Chicago], 1966), p. 10.

POLICE PROFESSIONALISM: DOES IT EXIST?

The move toward higher standards of police professionalism has come mainly from within the field, under the leadership of a relative handful of dedicated police reformers. At the national level, the FBI and the International Association of Chiefs of Police have provided leadership and assistance, and since 1965 the Justice Department's Office of Law Enforcement Assistance has played a growing role. But the concept of professionalism has not yet been adequately defined within the law enforcement community. The goal sought by some police officials seems to be a narrow one of administrative efficiency and organizational autonomy rather than a true sense of profession.

Some observers, therefore, have serious doubts about the objective of police professionalism. One scholar questions whether the police will ever be able to develop a true professionalism until the surrounding community ceases to view them as primarily responsible for catching criminals. As long as society tends to support managerial efficiency of the police over due process of law, an unhealthy tension will be generated between order and legality. This tension will only be resolved when the police role comes to be based more broadly on the values of a democratic legal order.[33]

Another scholar argues that a high level of professionalism in urban departments is unlikely because of the realities of the political process. He maintains that professionalism flourishes best under a nonpartisan government sustained by nonpartisan elites, which most cities are unable to maintain as they fill up with lower-income people and as the hostility of police-citizen contacts increases. Such a political climate is hostile to impersonal police efficiency, demanding control or influence over police behavior. The conditions of the central city generate other counterpressures to professionalism—not the least of which is the migration of

33. See Jerome H. Skolnick, *Justice without Trial: Law Enforcement in Democratic Society* (John Wiley & Sons, 1966), p. 239.

middle-income residents to the suburbs, bringing the prospect that "the tax resources necessary to support police work may decline at the same time that the cost of law enforcement rises." [34]

Another obstacle to professionalization of the police is the general failure to recognize the complexities of their role, particularly the important degree to which they exercise discretion in keeping the peace (see pp. 22–25). The tendency of the public and the police themselves to view their task as ministerial has been noted by observers,[35] and this view appears to many to disqualify them from professional status:

> One of the marks of a true profession is the inherent need for making value judgments and for exercising discretion based upon professional competence. To deny that discretion is exercised gives support to those citizens who maintain that the job of a police officer is a simple one, that it requires little judgment, and that it is not worthy of professional status.[36]

Acknowledgment of the large discretionary role involved in law enforcement is thus also a necessary precondition to professionalization of the police.

These doubts as to the desirability or feasibility of increasing police professionalism can probably be resolved by a better understanding of the police role on the part of both the public and the profession itself, but a radical change in commonly held views will be required.

The Police Role Reevaluated

If it is recognized that the predominantly peacekeeping function of the patrolman inevitably involves him in situations requiring delicate judgment, then it follows that he need not necessarily have "the expert aim of a marksman, the cunningness of a private

34. James Q. Wilson, "The Police and Their Problems: A Theory," *Public Policy*, Vol. 12 (1963), p. 214.
35. Wayne R. LaFave, *Arrest: The Decision To Take a Suspect into Custody* (Little, Brown, 1965), p. 510.
36. Goldstein, "Police Discretion: The Ideal versus the Real," p. 148.

eye, or the toughness of a stereotyped Irish policeman." Instead, he requires

> knowledge of human beings and the personal, as opposed to official, authority to influence people without the use or even threat of force. These characteristics are not commonly found in police officers because police departments do not consider these values as paramount....
>
> The image of police officers must be radically changed to consider them as a part of the broad category of occupations which deal with people who are sometimes difficult to handle.... If police work were seen in this light, individuals who were more sympathetic to human beings, and less prejudiced on racial or other grounds, would enter police work because they wanted to help human beings, instead of young men who are looking for excitement and the opportunity to exercise authority.... The heart of police work would be seen as consisting in work with difficult human problems by the majority of officers who would be recruited, trained, and promoted largely for this purpose.[37]

Three decades ago, August Vollmer propounded the same thesis. "Information now available indicates that the causes of crime are many, and that probably only concerted, coordinated action by all social agencies will reduce criminality," he argued. "The police, with all their opportunities for firsthand information, and their primary responsibility for protection of society against crime and criminals, must take the lead in community programs for crime prevention." He continued:

> The poor quality of personnel is perhaps the greatest weakness of police departments in the United States. In departments of all sizes, the percentage of men suited to police work is woefully small. ... The greater number of these men are badly placed and inadequately trained, yet they are charged with a task that would be difficult for men of the highest quality and skill.[38]

As the following chapter will show, much the same judgment can be made today. Although some states, regions, and individual

37. Bruce J. Terris, "The Role of the Police," *Annals of the American Academy of Political and Social Science*, Vol. 374 (November 1967), pp. 67–68.
38. Vollmer, *The Police and Modern Society*, pp. 3–4.

departments have made marked progress in elevating standards of personnel selection and training, police in the vast majority of agencies are poorly prepared for the difficult task they are expected to perform. As new demands and responsibilities are placed upon them, the difficulties are compounded by the general failure to understand and appreciate the complex nature of the police role and the high qualifications it requires.

CHAPTER THREE

The Police
Manpower Shortage

DECADES OF POLITICAL NEGLECT, public apathy, and professional parochialism have contributed to a growing shortage of police manpower throughout the country. The shortage is twofold:

Police agencies generally are understaffed and experiencing serious recruiting difficulties.

A significant percentage of the men on any force are not suited to meet the responsibilities of modern law enforcement.

These manpower problems are closely interrelated: the shortage of quantity cannot be solved, or even defined, without consideration of the shortage of quality. The need for higher police selection standards has been stressed for decades by the Federal Bureau of Investigation, the International Association of Chiefs of Police, and individual leaders in the field who have repeatedly warned that "the only way to improve law enforcement is to improve the law enforcement officer." [1] In other fields of public service it is accepted that the quality of services rendered is determined by the quality of the personnel who provide them. Nevertheless, the quality of police manpower has received scant

1. Southern sheriff quoted by Dana B. Brammer and James E. Hurley in "A Study of the Office of Sheriff in the United States Southern Region, 1967" (processed; University of Mississippi, Bureau of Governmental Research, 1967), p. 203.

attention. At all levels of government there is an evident reluctance to confront police personnel needs directly.

In part, this reluctance is rooted in one of the strongest traditions of the American constitutional system, under which "the prevention and punishment of crime in the streets is committed to state and local governments. It is essentially the task of mayors and local police, supported by their Governors." [2] This tradition presents a dilemma, for the scope of the problem delineated by the President's Commission on Law Enforcement demonstrates that the police function is no longer strictly a local and state concern. Indeed, the Omnibus Crime Control and Safe Streets Act of 1968 specifically declared that the incidence of crime "threatens the peace, security, and general welfare of the Nation and its citizens," and requires federal assistance, even while it affirmed that "crime is essentially a local problem." [3] Under this traditional formulation, it is difficult to discuss the deficiencies of the police on the floor of Congress. To do so is to attack the judgment and leadership of local officials from a national forum.

Ironically, the very fact of mounting public concern with "crime in the streets" poses a further obstacle to frank consideration of police manpower problems. Congressmen, anxious to be counted on the side of law and order, feel more comfortable defending the men in blue against their militant critics than exploring their deficiencies. Thus the legislative record contains little indication that critical problems actually exist but is punctuated with repeated expressions of praise and support for the police:

> I think we owe a great deal of gratitude to our policemen in our country because certainly conditions today make their job more dangerous and hazardous than ever before. These dedicated men should have our trust, confidence, and support in performing their

2. President Lyndon B. Johnson, "To Insure the Public Safety," Message on Crime to the Congress of the United States, Feb. 7, 1968, H. Doc. 250, 90 Cong. 2 sess. (excerpted in *New York Times*, Feb. 8, 1968).
3. P.L. 90–351.

duties, often without proper equipment and facilities, and nearly always without adequate compensation.[4]

Such statements serve to divert attention from the stubborn personnel deficiencies at the heart of the police problem. They suggest that there is a simple formula for law and order: trust the police, give them more equipment and higher salaries. But this appealing solution minimizes the magnitude of the problem and the difficulty and costs of achieving more effective law enforcement. Such formulas omit the ingredients which the President's Commission on Law Enforcement declared to be basic essentials: large-scale improvement in the strength and the caliber of police manpower.

The personnel needs which congressmen are so reluctant to face are documented in frank and repetitive detail in the files of the International Association of Chiefs of Police. The IACP has surveyed dozens of departments upon request, generally on a confidential basis. A sampling indicates why their findings are seldom released by local officials, and rarely come to public attention.

A *major southern city.* Training is minimal, caliber of personnel poor. "The average police officer in —— does not possess the skills and knowledge found in advanced and progressive police agencies in this country."

A *small New Jersey residential community.* "Deficient in almost every respect... pitifully poor number of applicants and qualified candidates." No oral interview is administered; no background investigation is made; virtually all applicants are accepted whether they pass the written test or not. Police chief attended school through eighth grade; three out of ten officers have attended the state police academy. "This lack of education and training becomes apparent during the examination of reports written by officers in the department. Only a few men can write passable reports; the remainder have difficulty expressing themselves and have problems with spelling and grammar."

A *well-to-do suburb in Massachusetts.* "Perhaps the most serious single deficiency of the —— Police Department is the lack of

4. Statement of Senator John L. McClellan, in *Controlling Crime through More Effective Law Enforcement*, Hearings before the Subcommittee on Criminal Laws and Procedures of the Senate Committee on the Judiciary, 90 Cong. 1 sess. (1967), p. 847.

supervisory and in-service training. Following selection, officers are sworn in, issued a sidearm and cartridges, and assigned to 'protect' the public." Quality of officers is below average; half have no more than a tenth-grade education. None have ever been fingerprinted; the background check is cursory. Town selectmen may waive the results of the entrance examination and often do. No members of the force have ever received outside training; field training is non-existent; no instruction is provided after recruit training. The overall department is unsatisfactory; its administration is ineffective.

A *major eastern industrial city*. "Frankly the ——— Department does not have a reservoir of educated and dedicated young officers with command experience to make maximum use of the many recommendations presented in this report." One-fourth of the force has no more than tenth-grade schooling. Present procedures do not obtain the best candidates: "75 percent pass the written test, a sure sign that it is too easy." Training is poorly administered, because of lack of competent staff, and is mainly limited to recruit training, which is inadequate. The curriculum is deficient on patrol methods, inspectional services, and field contact procedures. Field training is hit or miss; inservice training is only provided for juvenile and ambulance officers. No refresher training.

Such severe criticisms of police competence are rarely made in public by the law enforcement community. They are affirmed, however, in a growing body of literature by former officers writing out of apparent concern for the future of their profession. One such study describes how the closed police society tends to transform the best intentioned recruit into an authoritarian agent of control, driving the better-educated men into administrative or other duties and leaving the least desirable men out on the beat.[5] Another outlines the brutalizing process which all recruits are subjected to as they become exposed daily to the corruptions of the street and the men who patrol it.[6] Another concludes that a quality police system can only be built on revolutionary changes, including the recruitment of a new breed of individual and a

5. Arthur Neiderhoffer, *Behind the Shield: The Police in Urban Society* (Doubleday, 1967).

6. Gene Radano, *Walking the Beat: A New York Policeman Tells What It's Like on His Side of the Law* (World, 1968).

thorough weeding out of "the indolent, lacklustcr types who drift from job to job before taking root in the security of the police system . . . the 'gung-ho' bully to whom the authority of a badge and gun is a license to intimidate . . . the sadists and psychopaths whose present numbers have provoked calls for psychiatric screening of all applicants." [7]

Such criticisms cannot be dismissed as irresponsible or ignored as isolated findings based on expericnce in a few specific departments. Individually, the IACP surveys may identify "local problems," but collectively, together with the comprchensive data assembled by the President's Commission on Law Enforcement, they describe a manpower situation which is national in scope and critical in its urgency.

The Quality Problem

Proposals to improve law enforcement often focus on equipment (more patrol cars, tear gas, shotguns, or tanks), organization and management (relief from clerical and other nonpolice duties, more staff specialists, more systematic deployment of personnel), or policy (better community relations, recruitment of more Negroes, better procedures for hearing citizen complaints). The full range of such proposals is represented in the detailed recommendations made by the President's Commission on Law Enforcement. The commission warned, however, that all its recommendations were "predicated on the sharp improvement of the quality of police personnel from top to bottom." And, it stressed, "the police personnel need . . . found to be almost universal is improved *quality*." [8]

The quality problem is built into the police system at every level. It begins with inadequate standards of selection which

7. William Turner, *The Police Establishment* (G. P. Putnam's Sons, 1968), p. 25.
8. U.S. President's Commission on Law Enforcement and Administration of Justice, *The Challenge of Crime in a Free Society* (Government Printing Office, 1967), p. 107.

permit too many unqualified men to enter. It is extended by ineffective probation which permits such men to stay. It is perpetuated by inadequate training, from the recruit stage on up the career structure, which provides little means of developing the best men or improving the worst.

INADEQUATE SELECTION STANDARDS

The President's Commission Task Force on Police stated bluntly:

> Existing selection requirements and procedures in the majority of departments, aside from physical requirements, do not screen out the unfit. Hence, it is not surprising that far too many of those charged with protecting life and property and rationally enforcing our laws are not respected by their fellow officers and are incompetent, corrupt, or abusive. One incompetent officer can trigger a riot, permanently damage the reputation of a citizen, or alienate a community against a police department. It is essential, therefore, that the requirements to serve in law enforcement reflect the awesome responsibility facing the personnel that is selected.[9]

Selection standards seldom meet such requirements. One governor's study recently described state standards for police personnel as "more likely to attract the unfit" and reported that "a disturbingly large percentage of applicants are lacking in educational qualifications, are above the optimum age for entrance into police work, or possess employment records which raise serious questions about their suitability. . . ."[10]

Research has yet to determine reliable indicators of aptitude or predictors of success in police work. Nevertheless, selection requirements might reasonably be assumed to include sound character, emotional stability, and above-average intelligence. Such qualities, of course, cannot be measured with precision, but many

9. U.S. President's Commission on Law Enforcement and Administration of Justice, *Task Force Report: The Police* (Government Printing Office, 1967), p. 125.
10. "The Police in Massachusetts," Report by the Governor's Committee on Law Enforcement and Administration of Justice, Dec. 21, 1967 (processed), pp. 3, 11.

police departments scarcely attempt to measure them at all. Although a variety of useful tools and techniques for objective screening of personnel have been developed in recent years, their use is not widespread. Except for physical standards, most departments do not make a comprehensive evaluation of each applicant's suitability for law enforcement.

Character. The President's Commission on Law Enforcement recommended that all police departments use thorough background investigations and personal interviews as minimum techniques for screening applicants. Few departments now use these techniques systematically. Some do not conduct any background investigation; most simply make routine checks of local police records, FBI files, and references supplied by the applicant.[11] Credit records, former places of employment, and prior places of residence are often checked by mail rather than in person, which increases the risk of obtaining incomplete or faulty information. Departments which make thorough background checks find they produce higher rejection rates.

A majority of departments assess the character of applicants by means of personal interviews, whose reliability is critically dependent on the judgment and experience of the administering officials. When conducted by a carefully selected board of examiners, oral interviews result in a higher rate of rejections for character defects, emotional disturbances, and questionable motives. More typically, however, the interview may involve a relatively brief conversation with the local civil service examiner or police chief. A small minority of departments also give a polygraph examination. This controversial screening device is questioned by many authorities, but some users claim it identifies serious personality disorders and deviant behavior in one out of every three candidates

11. The *New York Times* of Aug. 30, 1968, reported that, as a result of pressures to increase police manpower, "more than 2,000 armed policemen have been sent out to duty on the streets of New York in the last eight months before being cleared by the detailed background investigation that normally precedes appointments to the force."

who have fulfilled all other admission requirements satisfactorily.[12]

Emotional Stability. Despite the commission's recommendation that all departments conduct thorough investigations of each candidate's emotional fitness, only about a quarter of all departments administer psychiatric examinations. Those that do report them helpful in weeding out the mentally unfit.[13] Psychological tests, such as the Minnesota Multiphasic Personal Inventory, administered by psychologists hired on a consulting basis to interview applicants, are also becoming an increasingly common practice in departments of all sizes. Where the various types of personality examinations are used, they have been largely successful in eliminating persons with mental disorders from those whose applications have been accepted. Studies in major cities which conduct psychological screening indicate that recruits tend to be better adjusted and more stable and to display better judgment than the general population. But a recent IACP survey points out that only 41 of 162 major law enforcement agencies administer such tests, and six still do not conduct personal interviews.[14]

Intelligence. Standard texts in the field estimate that an IQ of 110–120 (the high-average range for the general population) is a minimum requirement for effective police performance. It is difficult to judge the extent to which this requirement is met nationally, however, since most departments do not administer IQ tests.[15] Studies of individual departments have revealed a significant percentage of personnel below the 110–120 range.

12. Richard O. Arther, "Why Does Police Work Attract So Many Failures?" *Law and Order*, Vol. 12 (September 1964), pp. 62–69.
13. Of 760 persons tested by the Los Angeles Police Department over a four-year period, 11.3 percent were rejected for psychiatric reasons. Half of these were identified as latent or borderline psychotics and one-fifth as schizoid personalities. U.S. President's Commission on Law Enforcement, *Task Force Report: The Police*, p. 129.
14. Report on the effects of screening by Margaret H. Peterson and Fred D. Strider of the University of Nebraska School of Medicine at a conference on violence sponsored by the American Psychiatric Society and the American Medical Association, reported in *New York Times*, Nov. 17, 1968. The IACP data are from its *Police Personnel Selection Survey* (IACP, 1968).
15. Only 55 agencies in the IACP's *Police Personnel Selection Survey* listed an IQ test among their requirements.

Almost all departments administer some form of written test for the purpose of evaluating mental ability. Such tests, however, are usually geared to minimal educational levels,[16] and passing grades may be adjusted according to staffing needs of the moment.

Educational qualifications provide a rough but important index of intelligence, competence, and capacity to absorb professional training. The President's Commission on Law Enforcement recommended a baccalaureate degree for all police personnel as an ultimate goal. This recommendation has been criticized as unrealistic, since less than 10 percent of all policemen have a college degree, about half have had no post–high school education, and many of the latter group have not even completed high school. The commission recognized, however, that such a sweeping reform would take many years. In the interim, it urged that all departments require applicants to have both a high-school diploma and a demonstrated ability to do college-level work.[17] Commission studies found that the educational level of policemen was below that of the general population in some parts of the country, and that in many departments, particularly in New England and the South, a majority of policemen had not completed high school.

Low educational attainment may not necessarily reflect on an individual applicant's intelligence, although it is likely to signal other problems of personal or social adjustment. In a time when the preponderant majority of the population completes four years of high school and goes on to college, however, the generally low educational level of the nation's police has critical implications. Unless educational standards for selection rise substantially higher than the steadily rising level of schooling for the general

16. The Massachusetts Governor's Committee on Law Enforcement and Administration of Justice noted that its state's entrance examinations for police "measure only the ability of a candidate to memorize a State manual on specific knowledge of law, police procedures, and first aid. The fact that 34.4 percent of the applicants who passed the most recent police entrance examination had not completed high school is, the Committee feels, a disturbing comment on its quality" ("The Police in Massachusetts," p. 13).

17. U.S. President's Commission on Law Enforcement, *The Challenge of Crime in a Free Society*, pp. 109–10.

population, the police manpower situation can only grow worse as departments increasingly draw their recruits from the bottom half of the population in terms of ability.

VARIATIONS IN STANDARDS BY REGION AND POPULATION

While selection standards nationally may be characterized as low, wide differences exist among regions. A master's thesis completed in 1961 which analyzed these differences found that a twelfth-grade education was required by virtually all departments in the western states and by a small minority in New England (Table 1). In a composite rating of selection standards, the study ranked the departments of the western states well above all others and New England far below all the rest. Even in the

Table 1. Comparative Regional Ratings in 1961

Region	No preemployment residence check	12th-grade education required	Physical agility tests	Oral interviews	Recruit training (200 hrs.)	No veterans' preference	Applicant rejection rate	Total percentage points	Average rating for region	Rank order
	Percentage of cities responding on selected factors									
New England	12.7	18.1	72.4	32.2	20.1	15.2	66.8	237.5	33.9	9
Middle Atlantic	8.5	88.1	83.0	14.0	16.7	4.1	70.6	285.0	40.7	8
East North Central	16.9	59.3	22.0	70.0	28.8	13.0	85.2	295.2	42.1	7
West North Central	4.6	91.0	18.2	76.8	13.7	16.0	78.2	298.5	42.6	6
South Atlantic	50.0	76.5	14.7	37.8	35.4	47.7	76.3	338.9	48.4	4
East South Central	16.7	83.3	25.0	62.5	33.3	43.7	53.7	318.2	45.4	5
West South Central	60.0	85.7	26.7	64.7	59.9	35.2	75.1	408.3	58.3	3
Mountain	45.5	100	63.6	81.3	45.5	25.0	79.4	440.3	62.9	2
Pacific	63.8	97.9	78.7	81.5	55.3	12.9	89.1	479.2	63.4	1
National average	27.3	70.9	51.5	51.8	34.6	13.0	77.7	331.8	47.4	—

Source: George W. O'Connor, *Survey of Selection Methods* (International Association of Chiefs of Police, 1962), Table 8.

Pacific states, however, wide variations existed among departments, with many maintaining selection standards below those of the region as a whole.[18] Similar differences were found among cities of the same size. Departments in the largest cities ranked first in the composite standings (Table 2).

Table 2. Comparative Population Group Ratings in 1961

	Percentage of cities responding on selected factors								
Population group	*No preemployment residence check*	*12th-grade education required*	*Physical agility tests*	*Oral interviews*	*Recruit training (200 hrs.)*	*Applicant rejection rate*	*Total percentage points*	*Average rating for group*	*Rank order*
Over 1,000,000	50.0	75.0	75.0	50.0	100	80.2	430.2	71.6	1
500,000 to 1,000,000	40.0	40.0	30.0	36.4	80.0	76.3	302.7	50.4	4
250,000 to 500,000	52.6	94.7	68.4	70.0	52.6	83.9	422.2	70.3	2
100,000 to 250,000	24.5	71.4	57.1	54.8	48.9	69.3	326.0	54.3	3
50,000 to 100,000	29.7	66.2	51.4	48.3	20.3	70.9	286.8	47.8	5
25,000 to 50,000	22.8	72.1	49.4	52.5	12.7	75.3	284.8	47.4	6
National average	27.3	70.9	51.5	51.8	26.8	78.0	308.3	51.0	—

Source: O'Connor, *Survey of Selection Methods,* Table 9.

Similar regional and population differences in police educational levels are apparent in a more recent IACP study: the percentage of officers with only a grade-school education ranged from 12.37 in New England to 0.72 in the Pacific states; 50.88 percent in New England had only a high-school education as compared with 20 percent in the Pacific states; 4.37 percent in the East South Central states held a college degree, 25.27 percent in the Pacific states. Just 3.61 percent of the officers in cities of over 1 million people had only a grade-school education, 9.07 percent in cities of over 500,000. Officers with only a high-school education constituted 45.61 percent of those reporting from cities under

18. George W. O'Connor, *Survey of Selection Methods* (IACP, 1962).

50,000, 26.11 percent in cities of over 1 million. Degree holders were 5.19 percent of the force in cities of 50,000–100,000, 18.38 percent in cities of over 1 million.[19]

Such differences among regions and population groups, within a generally low range, attest to the national scope of the police personnel problem. If citizens throughout the country need higher quality law enforcement, they also need higher quality personnel to enforce the law from city to city and state to state.

Rejection Rates. The screening of police candidates is a process of selection by rejection. Nationally, 77.7 percent of all candidates are rejected. The Pacific Coast region is most selective, turning down nine out of every ten candidates, whereas almost five of every ten who apply in the east south central region are accepted.[20] Physical requirements are often unrealistically high, and undoubtedly contribute to high rejection rates, but other standards for screening tend to be unrealistically low. The fact that most candidates fail to meet even these low standards suggests the magnitude of the manpower problem. If the nation's police departments strengthen their screening procedures, rejection rates will rise higher and recruitment will become still more difficult, unless law enforcement agencies take the necessary steps to attract higher quality candidates. (It is important to note that departments which have raised their standards significantly have reported an increase in the number of qualified candidates applying. This has been the case in the Multnomah County, Oregon, Sheriff's Department, the first local agency to require a baccalaureate degree for appointment to deputy positions, and in several other departments with high educational qualifications.[21])

Inadequate Training. Selection standards clearly fail to screen out many poor prospects for police work. What of the training

19. Unpublished data from a 1968 IACP survey by Nelson A. Watson of 4,672 officers in 50 states.
20. O'Connor, *Survey of Selection Methods*, Table 8.
21. Their testimony is included in a book about the Multnomah experience by Donald E. Clark and Samuel G. Chapman, *A Forward Step: Educational Backgrounds for Police* (Charles C Thomas, 1966).

they receive once they are appointed to the force? Whatever his potential, the recruit is unlikely to know much about his job, with its myriad mechanical aspects, or the laws and customs of the community he is expected to police. Training is essential to develop his skills and his understanding of the complexities of law enforcement, and citizens who have need of his services have a right to expect such capabilities. Nevertheless, fewer than 15 percent of all agencies provide immediate recruit training; 51 percent report that they provide it "as soon as possible." [22] The President's Commission on Crime in the District of Columbia commented wryly on this widespread practice:

> The Department itself is implicitly disturbed by this policy; ticket books are not issued to new recruits at the time they are assigned to precincts. The rationale for this procedure is that these men have not sufficiently developed their judgment faculties to be issued these books. They are, on the other hand, issued weapons and ammunition.[23]

Sooner or later, recruits generally get some training: 68 percent of all agencies provide formal programs of at least a week; 3.5 percent (representing about one quarter of all officers) conduct training programs of more than eight weeks. A few of these programs are commendable, according to the President's Commission Task Force, but "it remains doubtful whether even a majority of them provide recruits with an ample understanding of the police task." [24]

Most departments provide far less than the four hundred hours of classroom work combined with carefully supervised field training which the commission recommended as an absolute minimum. Much of the training is poorly presented by unqualified instructors; often it is irrelevant to the realities of police work

22. George W. O'Connor, "Police Training," Report for the President's Commission on Law Enforcement and Administration of Justice (processed; IACP, 1966), Tables 9 and 10.

23. *Report of the President's Commission on Crime in the District of Columbia* (Government Printing Office, 1966), p. 175.

24. U.S. President's Commission on Law Enforcement, *Task Force Report: The Police*, p. 138.

and lacking in essential background information on the principles of law enforcement and the police role in the community.

Inadequate recruit training is compounded by an almost totally ineffective system of probation. Even if modern procedures for testing and evaluating personal characteristics were widely used by police departments, no screening devices are entirely reliable: some poorly suited candidates will inevitably be accepted. Theoretically, the probationary period is designed to identify and eliminate these incompetents. But only a few departments make even a pretense of further screening during probation.

Typically, recruits are not carefully supervised during probation, and no reports are made of their performance. In Washington, D.C., for example, "invariably, with the exception of obvious disciplinary cases and voluntary withdrawals, all those who start recruit training finish it. If examinations are failed, they are readministered until passed." [25] In three-quarters of all departments, the probationary period lasts only six months, as compared with the eighteen-month period of careful observation and evaluation recommended by the President's Commission on Law Enforcement. In many jurisdictions, moreover, civil service regulations protect incompetent recruits by requiring the same procedures for dismissal of probationers as for regular personnel.

Inservice training throughout a policeman's career is provided by only a handful of departments throughout the nation. The President's Commission stressed the need for at least one week a year, and for special incentives to policemen to continue their education and acquire additional skills.

THE OUTCOME: INADEQUATE PERSONNEL

Such low standards of selection and training inevitably make policemen of many men who are unfit for law enforcement. What proportion of police personnel is unfit? In the 1930s the Wickersham Commission declared that "the great majority of police

25. *Report of the President's Commission on Crime in the District of Columbia*, p. 178.

are not suited either by temperament, training, or education for their position," and in the same decade a sociologist estimated on the basis of intelligence tests in selected cities that "at least 75 percent of the policemen in the country are mentally unfit for their work." [26] In 1952 this estimate was revised downward by a police psychiatrist and professor of criminology at the University of California (Berkeley). On the basis of his finding that 25 to 40 percent of applicants who have passed physical and oral examinations are eliminated by psychological testing, he estimated that "similar percents must generally slip through" in jurisdictions which do not employ such tests.[27] Increasing use of psychological and psychiatric examinations have certainly reduced the percentage of incoming recruits who are mentally or emotionally unsuited for the job, at least in those cities conducting such tests.[28] But the President's Commission Task Force on Police, while hazarding no estimates of the current percentage of police who are unfit, concluded that "far too many" are incompetent and corrupt.[29] Available evidence suggests that such officers still make up a significant proportion of personnel.

One survey conducted for the task force in slum precincts of Washington, Boston, and Chicago found that "27 percent of all officers were either observed in misconduct situations or admitted to observers that they engaged in misconduct." [30] The researchers

26. National Commission on Law Observance and Enforcement [Wickersham Commission], *Report on Police* (Government Printing Office, 1931), No. 14, p. 58; Read Bain, "The Policeman on the Beat," *Scientific Monthly*, Vol. 48 (May 1939), p. 452.

27. Douglas M. Kelley, "Psychiatry in Police Recruitment," *Police Yearbook 1953* [International Association of Chiefs of Police], p. 198.

28. See note 14 above.

29. U.S. President's Commission on Law Enforcement, *Task Force Report: The Police*, p. 125.

30. *New York Times*, July 5, 1968. The survey was never released by the task force, and its report referred to the problem of police dishonesty in general terms: "... In some cities a significant number of officers engaged in varying forms of criminal and unethical conduct. ... Even in some of the departments where the integrity of top administrators is unquestioned, instances of illegal and unethical conduct are a continuing problem—particularly in slum areas, where the most incompetent officers tend to be assigned ..." (U.S. President's Commission on Law Enforcement, *Task Force Report: The Police*, p. 208).

believed that their findings understated the actual amount of police misconduct in the slums. Such behavior included shaking down traffic violators, businessmen, drunks, and deviants; stealing from burglarized establishments; taking bribes for returning stolen property, altering trial testimony, and protecting illegal establishments; and carrying extra weapons to plant on citizens killed or injured by police as "evidence."

The same researchers also observed one out of every ten policemen using improper or unnecessary force in carrying out his duties. A more recent newspaper survey concluded that police violence is "a serious problem in all major cities," unlikely to be solved without "major changes in the purpose, recruiting methods, training, organization and tactics of the police. . . ." [31]

Several of the task force studies for the President's Commission confirmed that racial prejudice is a marked characteristic of patrolmen in ghetto areas. One of the authors later told the National Advisory Commission on Civil Disorders:

> In predominantly Negro precincts, over three-fourths of the white policemen expressed prejudiced or highly prejudiced attitudes toward Negroes. Only one percent of the officers expressed attitudes which could be described as sympathetic towards Negroes. Indeed, close to one-half of all the police officers in predominantly Negro high crime rate areas showed extreme prejudice against Negroes.[32]

Other task force surveys found further indications of widespread personnel inadequacies. Patrolmen interviewed in Boston, Chicago, and Washington, D.C., were judged to have a seriously low degree of professionalization, measured by their general lack of interest in the values and goals of police work.[33] In Philadelphia,

31. David Burnham, *New York Times*, July 7, 1968.
32. Albert J. Reiss, Jr., quoted in *Report of the National Advisory Commission on Civil Disorders* (Government Printing Office, 1968), p. 160. More comprehensive evidence of widespread racial prejudice among police in eleven cities is presented in *Supplemental Studies for the National Advisory Commission on Civil Disorders* (Government Printing Office, 1968), p. 109.
33. Albert J. Reiss, Jr., "Career Orientations, Job Satisfaction, and the Assessment of Law Enforcement Problems by Police Officers," in *Studies in Crime and Law Enforcement in Major Metropolitan Areas*, Field Surveys III, Vol. 2, Prepared for the U.S. President's Commission on Law Enforcement and Administration of Justice (Government Printing Office, 1966).

where pressures to fill police manpower requirements were described as intense, marginal candidates were customarily accepted and only "out and out undesirable" candidates were rejected.[34]

Such findings focused on major urban departments, whose selection standards are generally higher than those in smaller cities or rural areas. They cannot be dismissed as isolated observations of the "local problems" of individual agencies. They are corroborated in the IACP surveys of departments of all sizes throughout the country and in a growing body of scholarly research into the need for higher quality personnel. One such study suggests that the predominantly lower middle-class background of police recruits makes them less sensitive to differences in perspective between themselves and other members of the heterogeneous urban population and less likely to appreciate the subtleties and qualifying conditions associated with substantive and procedural criminal law, while their relatively lower level of education makes them less able to absorb the classroom instruction that might supply some of the background they lack.[35]

The police personnel system itself is another source of weakness:

... The police force is simultaneously a pool from which the best men are promoted to other status and into which are deposited those police officers who have failed to meet the department's standards in other assignments. Inevitably, the patrol officers are not the men thought of within the department as being the best.... Yet these are the police officers who have the jobs which bring them most often into contact with the poor and the minority groups at a time of great tension in the community. Even worse, these are the men who affect, in the sharpest and most profound way, the attitudes of the minority groups toward the white world....[36]

34. Joseph D. Lohman and Gordon E. Misner, *The Police and the Community*, Field Surveys IV, Vol. 2, Report to the President's Commission on Law Enforcement and Administration of Justice (Government Printing Office, 1966), p. 184.

35. John H. McNamara, "Uncertainties in Police Work: The Relevance of Police Recruits' Background and Training," in *The Police: Six Sociological Essays*, ed. David J. Bordua (John Wiley & Sons, 1967).

36. Paul Jacobs, *Prelude to Riot: A View of Urban America from the Bottom* (Random House, 1966), p. 56.

But the inadequacies of police manpower cannot be blamed entirely on the system. The general public failure to appreciate the need for higher quality law enforcement personnel and the failure of their officials to insist on it are contributing factors. Lack of public esteem for the police role helps perpetuate low selection standards, which produce a low caliber of man on the beat, who succumbs more readily to degradation within the closed society of the police. One case study documenting this vicious circle concludes:

> The policeman uses violence illegally because such usage is seen as just, acceptable, and, at times, expected by his colleague group and because it constitutes an effective means for solving problems in obtaining status and self-esteem which policemen as policemen have in common. . . . It is a result of their desire to defend and improve their social status in the absence of effective legal means. This desire in turn is directly related to and makes sense in terms of the low status of the police in the community. . . .[37]

The problem of inadequate personnel is as unlikely to be solved by attacks on the police system as by staunch defense of the men in blue. What is required is frank recognition of the problem, as a basis for public understanding and support for improved standards of selection.

THE OUTCOME: INADEQUATE LEADERSHIP

The inadequacies of selection and training standards pose personnel problems extending up the career ladder into the executive ranks of police departments across the country. The police system has long resisted lateral entry of specialists or able men from other fields, requiring that all candidates start at the bottom regardless of their experience. The leadership of the profession today, therefore, is almost exclusively drawn from the recruits of several decades ago. The flaws inherent in such a system have long been apparent:

37. William A. Westley, "Violence and the Police," *American Journal of Sociology*, Vol. 59 (July 1963), pp. 34–41.

The police officer who has walked his beat as a patrolman, investigated crime as a detective, and managed the technical routine of stationhouse activity as lieutenant or captain, is not fitted by this experience to administer the complex affairs of a large police department.... Thief-catching is a highly technical and very important phase of police work, and skilled men should be engaged in it. But the training that creates proficiency in this line is not the training to produce an intelligent administrator.[38]

The Wickersham Commission in 1931 cited incompetent leadership as the primary factor in inefficient police administration, a weakness which the commission attributed directly to the selection process:

... Since recruits have as a rule had nothing more than elementary schooling, are usually without cultural background and without an adequate sense of the qualifications for the discharge of their duties, it follows that a large part of them are not likely to be and are not competent patrolmen.... And from that source must come the commanding officers and nearly always the chief.... No pains are taken ... to educate, train, and discipline.... That is only to say that the personnel of the police force at its inception and in its continuance has not the character and qualifications which its responsible duties require....[39]

The intervening decades have brought little change in the system, as one police official has regretfully noted:

The time-honored, uninspired path of promotion sees an administrator fish-laddering his way up through the ranks without being prepared in anything more than a "by chance" manner for the new and difficult responsibilities of successive commands. The consequence is that many of today's police commanding officers are simply promoted patrolmen, not professional administrators carefully prepared for demanding roles in the complex enterprise that is the hallmark of contemporary police work.[40]

38. Raymond B. Fosdick, American Police Systems (The Century Co., 1920), pp. 220, 222.
39. National Commission on Law Observance and Enforcement, Report on Police, p. 3.
40. Samuel G. Chapman, "Developing Personnel Leadership," Police Chief, Vol. 33 (March 1966), p. 24.

The Municipal Manpower Commission in 1962 identified police leadership as the weakest link in local government administration. As one evidence of this, the commission reported that two-thirds of all directors of public safety in large cities and about nine out of ten in smaller cities had not earned a college degree, in contrast to the markedly higher educational attainment of most executives of other municipal agencies.[41] More recently, the IACP has reported similar percentages, showing that 9.2 percent of police administrators have earned degrees and 33.6 percent have attended college.[42] The President's Commission on Law Enforcement recommended completion of four years of college as a minimum requirement for all supervisory personnel—a standard which has long been accepted for executives in other agencies of government. There can be no question that police administration, as one of the most demanding and challenging fields of public administration, demands equally high standards of leadership.[43]

The part incompetent leadership plays in the inadequacies of law enforcement can never be measured, but it must be large. Scholars of municipal government frequently cite police departments as prime examples of poor administration. One study describes the power of the police bureaucracy to block new ideas, and the tendency of its personnel system to limit the choice of key administrators and to bar innovators and specialists, as sufficient to frustrate the most determined and imaginative new police commissioner.[44]

Unenlightened leadership has certainly been a major obstacle to higher personnel standards. Many chiefs, with little education

41. Municipal Manpower Commission, *Governmental Manpower for Tomorrow's Cities* (McGraw-Hill, 1962), p. 136.
42. George W. O'Connor and Nelson A. Watson, *Juvenile Delinquency and Youth Crime: The Police Role* (International Association of Chiefs of Police, 1964).
43. Police represent 6.3 percent of public employees in local government (*Statistical Abstract of the United States,* 1967, p. 156) and 4.5 percent of local government expenditures (*County and City Data Book,* 1967, p. 5).
44. Wallace S. Sayre and Herbert Kaufman, *Governing New York City: Politics in the Metropolis* (rev. ed.; W. W. Norton, 1965), pp. 288–90.

themselves, are hostile to the idea of raising educational qualifications. One observer has noted the frequency of such statements as the following: "My men don't need no education," "I've gotten along for forty years without an education, I see no reason why they can't," or "If they know more than me, the mayor may make them chief." [45] Another has charged that the police service often rejects and repels professionally trained men because

> ... at top levels of the police service there are far too many ignorant, foolish, narrow minds that look down upon the educated careerist as a "wet behind the ears" neophyte. The American police system is in some trouble today, and a major cause of its problems is the fact that it is not too bright at top levels. [46]

The Quantity Problem

The general reluctance to confront the problem of police quality does not apply to the question of quantity. When public pressures mount to improve the adequacy of police protection, local officials customarily suggest that things would be better if they could have more policemen. Public and private groups investigating local crime almost invariably call for substantial increases in personnel.

The numbers of police have, in fact, increased steadily in recent years. But the increase has been only barely proportional to population growth, indicating that law enforcement capabilities generally have not been strengthened. Actually they may have been weakened, for the incidence of crime is accelerating faster than population growth, creating new demands for police services. In its annual reports on crime in the United States, the FBI has repeatedly expressed concern with the failure of communities throughout the country to improve their ratio of police

45. Vern L. Folley, "The Sphere of Police Education," *Law and Order*, Vol. 15 (February 1967), p. 21.
46. A. C. Germann, "Education and Professional Law Enforcement," *Journal of Criminal Law, Criminology, and Police Science*, Vol. 58 (December 1967), p. 608.

to population: for the last decade, the ratio has remained virtually unchanged at 1.7 officers to every 1,000 persons.

There is no magic formula to determine how many more police are needed. The appropriate strength of a community's force depends on many variables, not the least of which are the caliber and state of its training, and its organization and administration. Other factors include the size, density, and economic and social characteristics of the population, and the public services, climate, and geography of the area.

One city may require a police-population ratio considerably higher than the national average; another may function adequately with a much lower ratio. Ratios for cities with populations over 250,000 range from 1.1 to 4.1 per thousand, with an average of 2.7; for communities of fewer than 10,000 persons, 0.2 to 7.0, with an average of 1.5.[47] No correlation has been discovered between police-population ratios and the number of crimes committed or solved in the various cities, but it seems clear that most American communities do not have enough policemen.

THE CURRENT SHORTAGE

Perhaps the most realistic available measure of manpower need is the difference between actual strength, authorized strength, and the strength which law enforcement authorities consider appropriate. Nationwide, a National League of Cities survey indicates, police departments average 5 percent below authorized strength and 10 percent short of needed strength.[48] The reported need varies according to region and population category: cities in the South are 21 percent short, in the Midwest 13 percent, and in the Far West and New England 9 percent each. Large and small departments face similar shortages, with cities of over

47. *Uniform Crime Reports—1967* [Federal Bureau of Investigation], p. 44.
48. Raymond L. Bancroft, "Municipal Law Enforcement 1966," *Nation's Cities*, Vol. 4 (February 1966), pp. 15–26. The survey covered 284 cities of all sizes, representing about one-third of the nation's civilian and police population. The estimates, of course, represent only the best judgment of administrators, who would not be expected to underestimate their staff needs.

250,000 persons 11 percent below needed strength and cities of smaller size 17 to 19 percent. The President's Commission on Law Enforcement concluded: ". . . It is apparent that more police are needed and the municipalities must face up to the urgency of that need and provide the resources required to meet it if crime is to be controlled." [49]

FUTURE NEEDS

In the next decade, the police shortage seems certain to become more urgent. According to the Bureau of Labor Statistics, ". . . An estimated 15,000 opportunities will occur each year for qualified candidates to enter police work" through the 1970s.[50] This projection, however, was not based on need but on maintenance of the present police-population ratio.[51] If any progress is to be made toward reaching authorized or desired staffing, recruitment needs will be substantially larger. The President's Commission on Law Enforcement estimated that it would take 50,000 additional policemen simply to fill the positions authorized in 1967. To maintain the nation's police forces at strength thereafter would require the recruitment of roughly 30,000 men annually.

Even this estimate may be too conservative, in view of the likelihood that continued growth of urban populations, spiraling crime rates, and racial and other social unrest will require improvement in the police-population ratio. Moreover, the annual turnover rate is expected to increase in the next few years as the large numbers of men recruited in the years following the Second

49. U.S. President's Commission on Law Enforcement, *The Challenge of Crime in a Free Society*, p. 107.
50. U.S. Department of Labor, Bureau of Labor Statistics, *Occupational Outlook Handbook, 1968–69*, Bulletin No. 1550, p. 301.
51. Technical memorandum for BLS files by Joseph L. Rooney, Nov. 8, 1966. The projection also assumed an annual separation rate of 2.613 percent, the average rate for all service occupations. This assumption is decidedly conservative: the 1966 National League of Cities survey reported a 5.4 percent turnover rate for police due to death, retirement, and transfer to other occupations. The IACP describes a 5 percent turnover rate as low enough to indicate "the agency may be in danger of stagnation" ("A Survey of the Metropolitan Police Department, Washington, D.C.," in *Report of the President's Commission on Crime in the District of Columbia* [Government Printing Office, 1966], Appendix, p. 125).

World War reach retirement. The average age of 36 for police officers reported in the 1966 National League of Cities survey is an indicator of higher turnover ahead in what is essentially a young man's profession.

Manpower needs in the next decade will be further increased by any large-scale efforts to improve law enforcement. The President's Commission on Law Enforcement recommended establishment of three separate levels of entry: the paraprofessional category of *community service officer,* the *police officer* to serve routine patrol duties, and the *police agent* to perform a higher range of skilled tasks. Such restructuring of the police job and the recruitment of specialists from other fields such as law, sociology, psychology, and business, as suggested by the commission, would inevitably require more men.

Police needs in the next decade, then, would require at least doubling the number of young men annually recruited into the ranks. The magnitude of this task is evident when it is recalled that about four out of every five applicants for police work are rejected.

Quantity and Quality: Inseparable Problems

Individual communities, facing mounting pressures to increase the strength of their police departments, are frequently tempted to solve their recruitment problems by lowering selection standards. Invariably, such expedients only compound their manpower shortage. Acceptance of less qualified candidates drives the better men away, depleting still further the supply of competent applicants in the selection pool.

Baltimore in 1952, for example, lowered its requirement to an eighth-grade education or its equivalent, only to experience a dwindling number of applications over the next decade. In 1965 an IACP survey concluded that the city's recruiting problem was due in large measure to the lowered educational requirement, since "many prospective applicants who are high school graduates or who have had college training are unwilling to associate them-selves with a standard which is this low." [52] At the time of the survey 21 percent of the city's 3,000 sworn personnel consisted of men with an eighth-grade education or less, and 52.3 percent of the force had not gone beyond tenth grade. Moreover, the IACP noted, those with the least education tended to achieve the longest tenure in the department, since their lack of qualifications gave them less opportunity to move into other fields. By contrast, com-munities such as Multnomah County, Oregon, which have signifi-cantly raised entry requirements have found that the quantity and quality of eligible applicants have increased. [53]

Police manpower shortages will never be solved by choosing between quality and quantity; the question is how to obtain both. Unless efforts to recruit more men are accompanied by positive measures to attract better men and make the best possible use of their capacities, the result will be reduced police effectiveness.

OBSTACLES TO RECRUITMENT

No community acting alone can remove all the obstacles to recruitment of qualified police candidates in the numbers needed. The obstacles—low salaries, poor conditions of employment, and low public esteem—confront every department in the country, from the best to the worst.

Salaries. In few departments throughout the country are police salaries competitive with those in other occupations seeking men of ability and education. Median starting salaries for patrolmen range from $6,607 in smaller communities to $7,043 in cities of 250,000–500,000. By regions, they range from $5,214 in the South to $7,458 in the West. Maximums for patrolmen are only slightly higher: the median is $6,968 in smaller communities and $8,819 in cities of 250,000–500,000, and ranges from a low of $6,120 in the Southern states to a high median of $8,772 in the Western

52. "A Survey of the Police Department of Baltimore, Md." (processed; IACP, 1965), p. 172.
53. See note 21 above.

states. Median salaries for police chiefs range from $9,482 in smaller communities to $22,120 in the larger cities.[54] Fringe benefits for the police service are no longer superior to those in private industry. Most cities still maintain a single salary schedule for police and firemen, although they perform entirely different jobs requiring different orders of skill. (Significantly, fire departments have experienced few of the recruiting difficulties common to the police service.) Efforts to improve police performance will be futile until communities are willing to pay the price for major increases in police salaries.

Working Conditions. Poor working conditions and a regimented environment contribute to the difficulties of recruitment and retention, the President's Commission Task Force on Police reported. It found agencies generally working in cramped and badly maintained quarters, with deficient equipment and limited clerical help. Separate levels of entry and differentiation of the police role to provide more opportunities for specialized skills and other reforms of the closed personnel system were urged to improve the professional climate:

> Unnecessary regimentation should be removed, independent judgment should be encouraged, and criticism of existing practices should be solicited. Police departments traditionally have resisted change and have been wary of the intellectual. As long as this attitude prevails, the police will never successfully compete for the type of person they so desperately need.[55]

The Police Image. The other obstacles to recruitment are closely related to, and supported by, the low level of respect and understanding for the police and their task. The police image in the community at large contributes to a reluctance to improve their salaries and working conditions and exacerbates morale problems within their closed society:

54. *The Municipal Yearbook, 1969* [International City Management Association, Washington, D.C.], pp. 146, 148.
55. U.S. President's Commission on Law Enforcement, *Task Force Report: The Police,* p. 136.

Low salaries, along with inadequate equipment, run-down buildings, poor uniform allowances, and depressing squad rooms are obstacles in the way of effective police work mainly because they are interpreted by policemen as palpable evidence of the contempt in which the police are held by the public and the politicians. The police are starved for facilities and money, many policemen feel, because the public does not respect either law or law man.[56]

Salaries and working conditions are not likely to undergo major improvements until they are supported by the public. But local police, government officials, and community leaders have been notably unsuccessful in fostering recognition that "the investigation or prevention of crime, the protection or assistance of citizens, and the administration of a complex governmental agency all provide stimulating career opportunities for the talented and the educated."[57]

ASSESSING POLICE EFFECTIVENESS

Any discussion of problems of police quality and quantity is made more difficult by the inadequacies of existing criteria for evaluating police effectiveness. The usual measures—authorized strength, equipment, and trends in crime statistics—do not take full account of the realities of the police task and fail to measure the quality and competence of personnel.

Take, for example, the concept of authorized strength as an index of manpower needs. Manpower is unquestionably needed in greater numbers, but the actual need has little relation to authorized strength, which is an arbitrary figure set by local governments to approximate the number of officers the community can realistically afford (or *should* afford—lack of adequate appropriations is as much a factor in keeping units below strength as difficulty in recruiting). Police estimates of need are usually higher and are probably more realistic but scarcely more systematic.

56. James Q. Wilson, "The Police and Their Problems: A Theory," *Public Policy,* Vol. 12 (1963), p. 214.
57. U.S. President's Commission on Law Enforcement, *Task Force Report: The Police,* p. 134.

Estimates of future needs are generally derived by applying the current police-population ratio to the anticipated increase in population over time, but such ratios vary widely from one community to the next and appear to have little relationship to the crime index. There is no reason to accept any arbitrary manpower ratio as a basis for estimating future needs. Different organizational patterns produce different ratios, and there is no way to determine which pattern is best since organizational strategies depend crucially on the managerial skills at the top, the kinds of specialists available, and the competence of the ordinary patrolman.

The truth is that no one can say with certainty what numbers of men are needed to accomplish a major reduction in street crime. The question is academic anyway, since it is practically impossible to provide a constant police presence: the manpower requirements would be too great, and the costs would be prohibitive. However badly more officers may be needed, numbers alone will not solve the crime problem, as a former police commissioner of New York City has testified. The answer, he said, lies in

> a primary emphasis upon the quality of the police service rendered, which in turn will depend upon the caliber of person recruited to police work, on the scope of the education and training which that person will bring to his work, and on the direction and leadership which he receives.[58]

More manpower will not necessarily reduce crime, but it will greatly increase police expenditures, 90 percent of which are for personnel. Higher salaries will undoubtedly attract more men temporarily, but they are unlikely to be better men unless the salary increases are part of a comprehensive effort to improve selection standards, training, and opportunities for higher education. Until ways are found to measure the competence of police manpower, estimates of personnel needs will continue to be relatively meaningless. The question is not how many bodies, but

58. Vincent L. Broderick, in Hearings before the Subcommittee on Criminal Laws and Procedures of the Senate Committee on the Judiciary, July 12, 1967, *Controlling Crime through More Effective Law Enforcement*, 90 Cong. 1 sess. (1967), p. 1167.

how many trained men, are available. An understrength force of highly qualified men is preferable to an overstrength force of incompetents. As more states enact standards legislation and wider agreement is reached on the scope and content of training, it should become possible to analyze a given force in terms of "manpower fully qualified and trained." Only then will the statistics have meaning.

The relation of equipment and facilities to the effectiveness of a police force is more tenuous than numerical strength. Yet for decades, calls for better policing have been translated into more squad cars or motorcycle patrols, more sophisticated weaponry, and better facilities. One authority has sharply criticized the tendency of police commanders to measure their effectiveness in terms of equipment:

> The use of such measures of efficiency implies a feebleness in true administrative capacity that is all too often substantiated by the results of firsthand investigation. Moreover, a public necessarily unschooled in the realities of police duty often finds it easier to appraise its police defenses in terms of mere physical resources than in terms of the quality and discipline of officers and men. Here then is the problem represented by the mechanical device in police service: while it makes only minor and secondary contributions to police efficiency, it serves to divert attention of police and public away from those large issues of personnel management upon which success in police protection ultimately depends.[59]

While the police service must keep pace with developing technology, and while technology may alter manpower utilization, the effectiveness of manpower will always depend on the quality of the personnel.

Trends in crime statistics are widely noted by the public, and are perhaps the most commonly used index of police effectiveness. The steep and continuing rise in the national crime rate was repeatedly cited in congressional debate as a primary reason for the

59. Bruce Smith, *Police Systems in the United States* (2d rev. ed.; Harper & Row, 1960), p. 322.

legislation of 1968. At the local level, a statistical increase in the incidence of any crime may bring criticism of the police force.

Public sensitivity to the crime index poses a continuing dilemma for police administrators. An upward trend in the statistics may rally support for increasing the police budget, but it can just as readily be interpreted as evidence of police failure. Accordingly, citizen perceptions may influence the organization and operation of a department in ways which actually decrease efficiency. A single violent crime may cause a large-scale reassignment of men to the temporary neglect of other responsibilities for public protection. Intensive newspaper coverage of a certain type of crime or periodic demands for a crackdown on particular activities such as gambling or prostitution may divert police attention from more important enforcement problems until pressures ease.

The inadequacies of crime statistics are numerous.[60] They are readily susceptible to manipulation by the reporting agencies to protect or enhance their image. Even at their most accurate, they may produce a distorted picture of the crime problem as it actually exists, according to the President's Commission on Law Enforcement, since an overwhelming percentage of crimes are never reported to the police. The FBI has made diligent efforts to improve the accuracy of national statistics, but they still do not provide much of the information which is relevant to analysis of the crime problem. The commission suggested a number of major changes to provide more useful statistical indexes of crime trends and volume.

Even if all crimes were reported accurately, the statistics would still be a dubious index of police efficiency or effectiveness. To begin with, catching criminals and dealing with crimes after they have been committed are only a small part of the law

60. Some of the difficulties with crime statistics are discussed by Daniel Glaser, "National Goals and Indicators for the Reduction of Crime and Delinquency," *Annals*, Vol. 371 (May 1967), pp. 104–26. See also Daniel Bell, *The End of Ideology* (rev. ed.; Free Press, 1965), who suggests in Chap. 8, "The Myth of Crime Waves," that there is actually less crime in the United States than in the past and that the country is far safer and more lawful than popular opinion imagines.

enforcement task. Furthermore, the relationship between the quality and amount of police activity and the rate of crime or the conviction of offenders is not predictable. The size and quality of a police force may have comparatively little effect on the prevalence of crime compared with other factors such as size, makeup, and density of population, geography, climate, and economic and social characteristics of the region. Probably the chief factor is population—its age, sex, race, mores, and particularly its economic status. One scholar has suggested that urban crime is essentially a problem of class (not race) compounded by urban congestion. By this theory, police work is unlikely to alter the incidence or pattern of crime significantly until the ghettos are turned into suburbs.[61] As for the conviction and disposition of offenders—an area which many observers believe holds the greatest prospect for reducing crime—the responsibility here rests with the courts and the correctional system and not with the police (except to the extent that they perform incompetently in their initial collection of evidence, which again raises the question of personnel quality).

Because the crime rate is affected only marginally by police competence, it is sometimes argued that efforts to improve manpower are of little value and could not significantly improve law enforcement. But the very intransigence and complexity of the crime problem points to the contrary conclusion. The view that education and training are unimportant in fighting crime is a modern version of the notion that was outdated fifty years ago, that a strong body, a night stick, and a revolver are the only qualifications for policing.

Even in the narrowest construction of the police role as thief catcher, crime statistics have little value as a measure of efficiency. The capacities of the individual largely determine the level of performance. Policemen are not expected to arrest all suspects, prosecute them, convict them, and sentence them; no such system

61. James Q. Wilson, "Dilemmas of Police Administration," *Public Administration Review*, Vol. 28 (September–October 1968), p. 420.

ever existed. "The aim is not . . . statistically measurable efficiency but rather . . . intelligent and responsible exercise of discretion." [62] Statistical measures of "intelligent and responsible exercise of discretion" do not exist, nor are they likely to become available in the near future. When better measures of police effectiveness are devised, however, they could reasonably be expected to take into account the individual officer's qualities of mind and character and the adequacy of his training—just as departmental surveys by the IACP and studies by private consultants have been concerned with standards of recruit selection and training in measuring competent performance. [63] Better measures of effectiveness should also take into account the fairness with which the laws are administered for all citizens and the extent of police compliance with the rule of law, as well as provide more sophisticated indexes of crime control.

A National Manpower Problem

The problems of manpower quality and quantity described above transcend traditional concepts of local responsibility. The record shows that most local governments are unable or unwilling to recruit qualified men in the numbers needed or to train them adequately. Progressive municipalities may approximate their authorized strength from one year to the next by outbidding and raiding neighboring jurisdictions. But such patchwork efforts will not begin to meet staffing needs, which are soon expected to require a doubling of the men recruited annually. Furthermore, only larger communities have the manpower resources from which to recruit adequate numbers of qualified candidates and a budget of sufficient size to support a formal training program.

62. Frank J. Remington, in Editor's Foreword to Wayne R. LaFave, *Arrest: The Decision To Take a Suspect into Custody* (Little, Brown, 1965), p. xvii.

63. Improvement of police effectiveness may actually show a negative correlation to crime statistics, at least in the short run, since more competent police work is likely to produce an increase in the number of offenders arrested. It may also result in a higher rate of unsolved crime, since greater public confidence in the police may encourage reporting of a larger percentage of crimes actually committed.

But the deep-rooted tradition of local responsibility for law enforcement hinders recognition of police manpower deficiencies as a national policy problem. Public discussion tends to assume that the need for more policemen reported throughout the nation somehow remains a series of isolated "local problems." A citizens' committee studying Chicago's police needs recommended 1,500 more officers, without any indication that their recruitment might be of any concern, cost, or benefit to persons outside the city limits.[64] A presidential commission reporting that the shortage of police manpower in Washington, D.C., "must be viewed as an urgent problem" failed to suggest that the problem might have important implications for Maryland and Virginia suburbanites and for visitors to the nation's capital from all of the fifty states.[65] Even the President's Commission on Law Enforcement, after describing the police shortage as nationwide, could only bring itself to recommend that each municipality provide the resources required to meet its own needs.

Traditional patterns of thinking about law enforcement tend to obscure another highly significant aspect of the national manpower problem: the grossly unequal protection of the laws which citizens receive as a result of the wide variations existing in police standards and practices. As crime statistics dramatically demonstrate, enforcement is provided in different degrees according to place of residence, income, race, and other factors which are irrelevant to the obligations of justice and the needs of all citizens for protection.

Similar variables influence the treatment of those who come in contact with the law. In one city police are instructed to shoot looters on sight; in another the authorities declare, "I am not going to order a man killed for stealing a six-pack of beer or a

64. *Police and Public: A Critique and a Program*, Final Report of the Citizens' Committee to Study Police-Community Relations in the City of Chicago to Mayor Richard J. Daley, May 22, 1967 (n.p.).

65. *Report of the President's Commission on Crime in the District of Columbia*, p. 160.

television set." [66] Respectable suburbanites urge that looters from the ghetto be shot, but no one suggests the same treatment for middle-class teenage shoplifters who account for far greater losses. Juveniles, in fact, account for over half of all crimes, and experts believe that the treatment they receive is the most important key to crime reduction. Few police agencies, however, handle the same kinds of juvenile cases in the same manner. In some communities the percentage of arrested youths referred to the courts is almost zero, in others almost 100 percent.[67] Civil rights demonstrators or protesting college students may be treated circumspectly, clubbed, or shot in the back according to the mores of the particular community and the inclinations of the local police.[68]

Varying standards of justice across the land have been tolerated throughout history without serious strain to the body politic, but they pose new dangers in today's society of instant communica-

66. Major General George Gelston, commander of National Guard forces in Cambridge, Md., in 1967, quoted in the *Report of the National Advisory Commission on Civil Disorders*, p. 176. Chicago Mayor Richard J. Daley's orders to city police to shoot arsonists and looters was reported in *New York Times*, April 16, 1968.

67. "Obviously, variation in police practice greatly determines the input of the courts" and therefore the kinds and degree of treatment received (Daniel Glaser, "National Goals and Indicators for the Reduction of Crime and Delinquency," pp. 121–22).

68. James Q. Wilson, in *Varieties of Police Behavior: The Management of Law and Order in Eight Communities* (Harvard University Press, 1968), generalizes that there are three basic styles of policing which vary in degree according to the political and social mores of the community. The *watchman* style emphasizes maintenance of order over law enforcement, ignoring or treating informally certain types of violations. Such departments are characterized by low standards of professionalization and a concept of the job as craftlike in character, learned by apprenticeship. Distributive justice is the standard for handling disorderly situations: police actions tend to be taken on the basis of a judgment as to what a person "deserves." The *legalistic* style places more emphasis on enforcement, issuing traffic tickets at a high rate, arresting a high proportion of juvenile offenders, and making a large number of misdemeanor arrests when the public order has not been breached. Discretion is deemphasized; strict enforcement of a single standard of behavior for the entire community is stressed. Such a style is often an outcome of reforming a previously corrupt department. The *service* style is characteristic of homogeneous middle-class communities in which there is high agreement on the need for and definition of public order but no administrative demand for a legalistic style. The emphasis is on protecting the community from minor and occasional threats posed by unruly teenagers and "outsiders." The character of the community permits the police to concentrate on managing traffic, regulating juveniles, and providing services.

tions and growing unrest. When civil disorders and violence strike hundreds of communities (and within a twelve-month period two national commissions are appointed to search out the causes) and when the capacity of local governments to maintain civil peace is seriously questioned, a new urgency attaches to the competence and fairness of law enforcement.

CONGRESSIONAL CONSIDERATION OF POLICE PROBLEMS

The need to upgrade the professional quality of state and local police forces was a central finding of the U.S. Commission on Civil Rights in 1961. Its primary recommendation was

> that Congress consider the advisability of enacting a program of grants-in-aid to assist State and local governments, upon their request, to increase the professional quality of their police forces. Such grants-in-aid might apply to the development and maintenance of (1) recruit selection tests and standards; (2) training programs in scientific crime detection; (3) training programs in constitutional rights and human relations; (4) college level schools of police administration; and (5) scholarship programs that assist policemen to receive training in schools of police administration.[69]

Several bills were introduced to carry out the commission's recommendation, without success. The idea did not receive the support of the administration until 1965, when President Johnson asked Congress to "bolster present training programs for law enforcement personnel and . . . support the development of new training methods." [70]

Spokesmen for the administration emphasized the limited nature of the bill, assuring Congress that it would only provide "selective support for model programs, programs to show what is possible. . . . That is the role we see for the federal government

---

69. *U.S. Commission on Civil Rights Report*, Bk. 5: *Justice* (Government Printing Office, 1961), p. 112.

70. Lyndon B. Johnson, "Law Enforcement and the Administration of Justice," Message to the Congress of the United States, March 8, 1965, H. Doc. 103, 89 Cong. 1 sess.

under this measure." [71] On this basis, the Law Enforcement Assistance Act of 1965 passed without controversy or fanfare and with only the briefest debate.

Grants and contracts for 359 separate projects totaling $20.6 million were awarded during the act's three years of existence. Some $13 million, or 63 percent, went to the field of law enforcement, with the rest allocated to the correctional system, courts, and other criminal justice agencies. The bulk of the $13 million went for projects designed to improve police methods and techniques. Only $4.4 million went to support training programs and $1.4 million for college-level educational programs for police.[72] The act demonstrated the potential value of federal aid for local law enforcement and the futility of such limited assistance. Grants awarded to establish degree programs were a major factor in the rapid expansion of college-level courses for police. Awards made to establish standards and training commissions in 22 states laid a necessary basis for the future improvement of training systems. Other grants supported a variety of state and regional projects to improve training and also some useful research on training needs and problems. On the other hand, the demonstration projects benefited few policemen directly. Grant recipients included over 100 educational institutions or state governments and only 11 local departments.

As crime became a paramount domestic issue, the Ninetieth Congress shifted the focus of the federal role. Acting on the findings of his commission on law enforcement, President Johnson in 1967 called for "an unswerving commitment by all levels of government to an intensified, long-term program of action." [73] He proposed grants to states and local governments for compre-

71. Attorney General Nicholas deB. Katzenbach, statement in Hearings before a Subcommittee of the Senate Committee on the Judiciary, July 22, 1965, 89 Cong. 1 sess. (1965), p. 7.
72. Department of Justice, Office of Law Enforcement, LEAA Grants and Contracts, Fiscal 1966–1968, Complete List of Project Awards under the Law Enforcement Assistance Act of 1965 (1968), p. i.
73. Lyndon B. Johnson, "War on Crime," Message to the Congress of the United States, Feb. 6, 1967, H. Doc. 53, 90 Cong. 1 sess.

hensive planning and action grants to stimulate new approaches and improvements in law enforcement and criminal justice. Action grants were recommended for a variety of purposes, such as purchase of equipment and support of projects to improve police management and organization, operations and facilities, and manpower, "including the recruitment, education and training of all types of law enforcement and criminal justice personnel." [74] But the request for $50 million for first-year appropriations contained no assurance that any of it would go to education and training.

Throughout extensive hearings held by two congressional committees on this and related bills, no one inquired what funds would or should be allocated to police education and training. In the House, Subcommittee No. 5 of the Judiciary Committee took 1,551 pages of testimony, but the bulk of it dealt with other issues such as wiretapping, firearms control, and the impact of Supreme Court decisions on law enforcement. Attorney General Ramsey Clark was questioned at length on these subjects. In his opening presentation he referred to the need for more and better police, but he never got a chance to amplify the point.

Detroit Police Commissioner Ray Girardin declared that all police departments need "training, training and more training" and that "inservice teaching and training is more desperately needed than ever in history." [75] But the committee gave no indication that it had heard his message. Nor did the members comment on the caveat expressed by Maryland Governor Spiro Agnew in his statement supporting the bill: "I cannot help but feel that we are overlooking the nuts and bolts of this problem. We should be putting more and better qualified law enforcement officers on the street. . . ." [76] The hearings concluded without further discussion of "the nuts and bolts," although Representative Richard H. Poff (Republican of Virginia) had earlier also raised a question about priorities:

74. H.R. 5037, 90 Cong. 1 sess. (1967).
75. *Anti-Crime Program*, Hearings before Subcommittee No. 5 of the House Committee on the Judiciary, 90 Cong. 1 sess. (1967), pp. 437, 439.
76. *Ibid.*, p. 444.

The first link in that chain [of priorities], it seems to me, is education and training of law enforcement officials and criminal justice personnel. Ask any police chief and he will tell you what he needs most is better trained men. The Commission agrees. The President agrees. The Justice Department, acting under the Law Enforcement Assistance Act, already has basic statutory authority to proceed. Rather than launch a new experiment with some untried program, we should invest whatever education and training money we can afford in prudent expansions of the Law Enforcement Assistance Act.[77]

In the Senate, hearings were conducted by the Subcommittee on Criminal Laws and Procedures of the Committee on the Judiciary. A statement filed by Senator Joseph M. Montoya (Democrat of New Mexico) on the opening day posed a provocative challenge to its deliberations:

Let us inquire into the caliber of personnel now being attracted into law enforcement. Where are the college graduates? The skilled and increasingly educated officers and research people? The criminal is smarter and tougher nowadays than his counterpart of previous eras. Why not the officer?

We must enable persons to further their education through police work. If we establish a series of educational incentives, it is conceivable that many young men will enter the field of law enforcement in order to better themselves, rather than because they cannot find anything else....[78]

But the proposed inquiry was never made. The closest approach to it came in a brief appearance by Senator Joseph D. Tydings (Democrat of Maryland) to support his own bill to provide grants for purchase of equipment and for education and training of police personnel. Tydings observed that the bill

deals with an important but little discussed aspect of the law enforcement problem; that is, the provision of adequate education and educational opportunities for members of our state and local police forces across the United States.... No task seems too difficult, too dangerous, or too discomforting to ask a policeman to do it. Yet the average policeman ... has at best a high school education.

77. *Ibid.*, p. 144.
78. *Controlling Crime through More Effective Law Enforcement*, p. 144.

In a nation which prides itself on having the world's best and most universally accessible school system, in which nearly 25 percent of its people finish college, we make the job of protecting society so unattractive that college graduates will not enter into it, and we pay so little for police work that those engaged in it can ill afford to pay their own way for further education. We must provide means for members of our police forces to further their education while members of the force, and incentives for college graduates to enter law enforcement work.[79]

Subcommittee Chairman John L. McClellan (Democrat of Arkansas) expressed interest in educational grants if they could be tied to law enforcement careers. He asked Tydings to submit written answers to questions about the proposal, which the Justice Department opposed on the grounds that the administration bill was more comprehensive. Tydings' memorandum argued that his measure was "far superior" in providing extensive assistance for police education, since the administration bill "provides little or no emphasis upon or explicit assistance to law officer education." [80] But no further testimony was taken as to the need for police education. In fact, legislation dealing exclusively with education for police was not even before the committee. An ambitious proposal for a law enforcement education act, a four-year $100-million program of college loans, scholarships, and fellowships for preservice and inservice personnel, had been introduced in the House by Representative William R. Anderson (Democrat of Tennessee), and a companion measure had been sponsored in the Senate by Abraham A. Ribicoff (Democrat of Connecticut), but both bills were referred to the education committees, where they died without hearings. They were never formally considered by the judiciary committees which framed the eventual legislation.

Training received somewhat better treatment in the Senate hearings. Detroit Police Commissioner Girardin was questioned

79. *Ibid.*, p. 855.
80. *Ibid.*, p. 860.

at greater length than during his appearance in the House. Senator McClellan asked him to identify the highest priority of need:

MR. GIRARDIN: No. 1, training.

SENATOR MC CLELLAN: Training?

MR. GIRARDIN: Yes. No police department can have enough training. We need training, training, and more training, both before the man becomes a police officer and while he is in service. I would say this would be No. 1.[81]

Attorney General Clark told the committee that "manpower, quality of manpower, standards for manpower, training, are primarily important" [82] and submitted a detailed memorandum singling out "training and education" as the top priority for action grants. His memorandum also noted that scholarship and fellowship grants could be provided under the administration bill as "special projects." [83] As in his House appearance, however, most of his testimony was consumed with questions about wiretapping, gun control, and the effect of Supreme Court decisions on interrogation of suspects and the admission of evidence.

As debate on the House bill began, Representative William M. McCulloch (Republican of Ohio) complained that the House had "not provided [police] with the education and training necessary to effectively perform their duties." [84] But the subject of education was never mentioned again throughout the three days of floor discussion. One amendment to strengthen training was accepted. Robert McClory (Republican of Illinois), observing that

81. *Ibid.*, p. 310. McClellan never accepted the chief's order of priorities, as he indicated later in the hearings. Training might indeed make "a substantial contribution," he allowed, "but if we cannot interrogate suspects and some policeman happens to stumble just a little in some ritual that is supposed to be used and by reason of that the guilty is turned loose, that will not develop strong law enforcement and will not improve conditions that now exist very much, if any" (*ibid.*, p. 561).

Richard Harris, in "Annals of Legislation: The Turning Point," *New Yorker*, Dec. 14, 1968, suggests that McClellan's primary motivation in conducting the hearings was to launch a concerted attack on the Supreme Court, using the growing unpopularity of court decisions in criminal cases to give it a thrashing for its decisions in civil rights cases.

82. *Controlling Crime through More Effective Law Enforcement*, p. 370.

83. *Ibid.*, pp. 830, 832.

84. *Congressional Record*, daily ed., Aug. 2, 1967, H 9793.

"adequate training of law enforcement officers is at the very foundation of improved law enforcement, respect for the law, and improving both the caliber and prestige of law enforcement officers across the land," proposed a national institute to conduct research and training programs.[85] This institute was to have authority to establish national or regional training centers, thus opening the possibility of systematic training on a nationwide basis. His colleagues passed McClory's amendment, after some questioning of the value of research, and proceeded to issues of apparently greater urgency.

Expressing distrust of federal involvement in local police affairs and lack of confidence in Attorney General Clark, they altered the grant proposals to provide block grants to the states. They directed that "highest priority" be given to controlling riots and combating organized crime and raised the authorization to $75 million, specifying that $30 million of it be allocated for these purposes. After a round of oratory berating the Supreme Court for "coddling criminals" and inveighing against "crime in the streets," the bill was passed without further discussion of police manpower needs.

The Senate did not get around to anticrime legislation for another ten months. In the interim, the administration had made some changes in its original recommendations. President Johnson doubled the first-year appropriation request for his crime control bill to $100 million and added four new provisions "because . . . training and education are so essential. . . ." [86] He asked for expansion of FBI training activities; "more substantial financial assistance to state and local law enforcement agencies to develop their own training programs"; a program of fellowships, loans, and tuition aids for local law enforcement officials (similar to that proposed in the Anderson-Ribicoff bill); and creation of a national institute of law enforcement and criminal justice (with

85. *Ibid.*, Aug. 3, 1967, H 9892.
86. "To Insure the Public Safety," Message on Crime to the Congress of the United States, Feb. 7, 1968.

authority to conduct and sponsor research but no power to establish regional training institutes, as proposed in the McClory
amendment which the House had accepted).

The President's request for educational assistance reflected
Congressman Anderson's persistence more than a systematic reordering of priorities within the executive branch. Frustrated in
his efforts to obtain congressional consideration, he had shifted
his attention to the White House. Fortuitously, he was instru-
mental in persuading the President to address the IACP's 1967
convention in Kansas City, where on September 14 Mr. Johnson
delivered a strong speech urging a national policy against crime.
The speech was widely applauded, and the President was grateful.
When he subsequently received a memorandum from Anderson
spelling out the case for a law enforcement education bill (with
an extensive list of mayors, police chiefs, and others who endorsed
it), he directed his staff to add it to the other amendments recommended by the Justice Department for inclusion in the 1968
recommendations.

By the time it was reported to the Senate floor, however, the
administration's relatively simple grant program had been trans-
formed into an omnibus crime-control measure—or, as some
described it, a "Christmas tree bill" loaded with additional pack-
ages. Johnson's recommendations survived substantially intact as
Title I. The Judiciary Committee doubled the first-year funding
authorization, accepted the research institute and a modest program of academic grants and loans on the Anderson-Ribicoff
model, but rejected a general support program to help local agencies improve their training, providing instead for a major expansion of FBI training activities for state and local police.[87]

These changes were hardly noticed, however, in the controversy over three other titles in the omnibus bill. One, designed to

87. This section was inserted as a result of FBI lobbying to extend its control
over police training and in spite of the opposition of the IACP, which feared that
centralized control of training by the FBI would be a dangerous step toward a national police force. See Drew Pearson, *Washington Post*, Feb. 17 and April 16,
1968.

overturn Supreme Court decisions on the inadmissibility of confessions as evidence, provoked wide opposition from constitutional lawyers and civil libertarians. Another, providing broad authorization for wiretapping by law enforcement personnel, was strongly opposed by the administration. A third, a watered-down version of the administration's gun control bill, was contested by some who thought it went too far and others who thought it did not go far enough.

"The only part of this measure that is likely to do anything to make the streets safer is Title I," Senator Wayne Morse (Democrat of Oregon) advised his colleagues as debate opened.[88] But Title I was virtually forgotten for most of the seventeen days of debate. After limiting the authority of the attorney general by approving a block-grant amendment similar to that passed by the House, the Senate left Title I relatively intact and moved on to the other titles, adding several more before the bill was passed.

In an emotional session following the assassination of Senator Robert F. Kennedy, the House voted to speed passage of anti-crime legislation by taking up the Senate omnibus bill instead of sending the conflicting measures to conference. A few congressmen protested the Senate provisions on wiretapping and use of confessions, and Representative Celler warned that the entire bill was "a cruel hoax,"[89] but they were ignored in the rush to "do something" about crime and violence. As the House overwhelmingly voted passage, Representative Henry S. Reuss (Democrat of Wisconsin) warned: "If we are serious about controlling crime in this country, we should start again, and do it right. . . ."

The solution to the problem of crime and violence does not lie in the direction of allowing underpaid and ill-trained policemen to take shortcuts to law and order by depriving us of both our privacy and our constitutional rights. Rather, we should pay the price necessary to obtain men of ability in sufficient numbers and sufficiently

---

88. *Congressional Record,* daily ed., May 2, 1968, p. S 4853.
89. *Ibid.,* June 5, 1968, p. H 4556.

well paid, to assure that not only order, but the quality and character of our society, is preserved.[90]

His words underlined what the legislative record reveals: that at no point in the development of the act did the Congress consider how to meet the critical manpower problems identified by the President's Commission on Law Enforcement. The lawmakers ignored the commission's emphatic finding that "widespread improvement in the strength and caliber of police manpower, supported by a radical revision of personnel practices, are the basic essentials for achieving more effective and fairer law enforcement." [91] Instead, Congress placed its emphasis on technology and equipment, riot control, combating organized crime, and loosening restrictions on police operations to achieve the stated objective of "strengthening and improving law enforcement at every level." [92]

The potential impact of the programs established by the Omnibus Crime Control and Safe Streets Act of 1968 will be assessed in the following chapters. However beneficial they may be, they cannot be said to deal directly with the inadequacies of police personnel. The act fails to recognize that the deficiencies reported by the President's Comission constitute a manpower problem of national dimensions—one that requires national programs and policies to overcome the reluctance of able young men to enter the police service and to provide them with adequate training throughout their careers.

At a time of nationwide demands for better law enforcement, the question may well be asked: How much injury will society suffer, how costly must the consequences be, before adequate policies are developed and the necessary resources mobilized to solve the growing crisis of police manpower? The next three chapters suggest the kinds of national policies needed and the resources they will require.

90. *Ibid.*, June 6, 1968, p. H 4637.
91. U.S. President's Commission on Law Enforcement, *The Challenge of Crime in a Free Society*, p. 294.
92. P.L. 90–351.

CHAPTER FOUR

Education for Policemen

ALTHOUGH MANY of its recommendations could be put into effect relatively quickly, given enlightened leadership, the President's Commission on Law Enforcement spoke in long-range terms in dealing with police education: "The ultimate aim of all police departments should be that all personnel with general enforcement powers have baccalaureate degrees." [1] Two questions are posed by this recommendation: Is it realistic, and is it really necessary? Neither question has yet been adequately explored, and the commission's specific proposal has been generally ignored or dismissed as impractical. Similar proposals have been made before (although never by a major federal commission), and they have been accorded the same fate.

Dismissal of the proposal as unrealistic, however, ignores the commission's explicit recognition that many years would be required to implement the standard and its carefully considered recommendations for interim steps. It urged that modest reforms be undertaken at once: police departments should insist that all recruits have a demonstrated capacity for college-level work and that all candidates for police agent have at least two years of college. Four-year degrees should immediately be required for police chiefs and made a short-range requirement for supervisors and administrators, with the long-range objective of requiring all high-

1. U.S. President's Commission on Law Enforcement and Administration of Justice, *The Challenge of Crime in a Free Society* (Government Printing Office, 1967), p. 109.

ranking officers to have advanced degrees in law, sociology, criminology, public administration, or some other appropriate specialty.

The goal of a four-year degree is beyond the reach of perhaps two out of every three officers currently employed. The possibility of its being achieved substantially with present personnel exists only in the Pacific states, where an estimated 25 percent of police already have college degrees and another 54 percent have some post–high school education. Throughout the rest of the country, only about 5 percent of police are college graduates. In the eastern states, a majority have not had any higher education; roughly 15 percent have not even finished high school.[2] Among the nation's sheriffs, educational attainment is lower: 24 percent have not finished high school, 42 percent have received a diploma, and 34 percent have had some higher education.[3] In southern states, the picture is worse: 39.7 percent of the sheriffs have not completed high school, and only 20.8 percent have had some higher education.[4] Clearly, revolutionary changes in recruitment and staffing would have to take place in order to reach the commission's proposed educational goal for the nation's police. Some scholars who are fully aware of the dimensions of the manpower problem are doubtful that the result would be worth the effort required. One, noting that "it is not yet clear exactly in what ways, if at all, middle-class, college-educated men make better police officers," has expressed the pessimistic view that such persons are unlikely to be interested in a police career and that, even if they were, not enough could be attracted to fill more than a fraction of the total numbers needed.[5]

2. Unpublished data from a 1968 IACP survey by Nelson A. Watson of 4,672 officers in 50 states.
3. Stanley E. Grupp, "Work Release—the Sheriff's Viewpoint," *National Sheriff*, March–April 1968.
4. Dana B. Brammer and James E. Hurley, "A Study of the Office of Sheriff in the United States Southern Region, 1967" (processed; University of Mississippi, Bureau of Governmental Research, 1967), p. 50.
5. James Q. Wilson, *Varieties of Police Behavior: The Management of Law and Order in Eight Communities* (Harvard University Press, 1968), p. 281.

But the commission's recommendation is not as unrealistic as it may seem. The police and the academic community are already being drawn into closer relationships. Law enforcement degree programs have developed rapidly in recent years and in 1968 enrolled some 32,000 students in 234 separate educational institutions. Almost half of these students are inservice policemen who recognize the value of higher education for advancing their careers. The other half represent a potential source of qualified manpower which the police service must learn to attract.

The alliance between the colleges and the police is still relatively new and often shaky, but it may prove highly significant for the future of law enforcement. This chapter will consider the case for higher education of police, examine the kinds of college-level programs now available, and explore the probable effects of implementing the commission's recommendation on the academic community, the police, and the nation.

Why Higher Education for Police?

Do police need a college education? Does it really pay off in terms of better law enforcement? Some of the nation's most respected law enforcement units—the Federal Bureau of Investigation and the Secret Service—answered these questions to their own satisfaction several decades ago. They and other federal investigative agencies have long insisted on the baccalaureate degree as a minimum requirement for their agents. But the police service at the municipal level has not accepted this standard, even though local law enforcement may well be a more demanding occupation—"far more complicated, technical, and of far greater importance to the American way of life than is the federal service." [6]

The reasons advanced for college education for police are essentially the same as those used to justify higher education as

6. E. Wilson Purdy, "Administrative Action To Implement Selection and Training for Police Professionalization," *Police Chief*, Vol. 32 (May 1965), p. 16.

preparation for any other career. They rest more on faith than on fact. Evidence does not firmly establish the necessity of four years of college for entry into any field: research is unable to determine how much knowledge college graduates retain from their studies or even whether their personalities and values are significantly altered by the process.

Nevertheless the worth of a general collegiate education for all youth of intelligence and ambition is unquestioned, and the role of the four-year liberal arts college in providing it generally accepted as essential. Sociologists point out that this role has important functions beyond the development of talented manpower. The liberal arts education provides "ethical and moral indoctrination that legitimizes existing power arrangements, and reinforces appropriate attitudes for the sustenance of democratic institutions and the peaceful coexistence of diverse population groups." Moreover, it serves as

> a constituent element in all scientific, professional, and management training and as such is presumably directly instrumental in enhancing occupational competencies. In one sense general education is the most efficient form of occupational training. Rapid change is hostile to narrow expertise and a curriculum that emphasizes breadth and flexibility may better equip students to meet unpredictable vocational demands.[7]

These functions, important in the preparation for many occupations, are especially relevant in the case of the police, who bear a unique responsibility for maintaining democratic institutions and assuring the "peaceful coexistence of diverse population groups." Police work, moreover, is obviously susceptible to "unpredictable vocational demands."

The qualities which law enforcement leaders claim to look for in recruits are the very ones which liberal education is believed to nurture: knowledge of changing social, economic, and political conditions; understanding of human behavior; and the ability to

7. Marvin Bressler, "Sociology and Collegiate General Education," in *The Uses of Sociology*, ed. Paul F. Lazarsfeld, William H. Sewell, and Harold L. Wilensky (Basic Books, 1967), p. 50.

communicate; together with the assumption of certain moral values, habits of mind, and qualities of self-discipline which are important in sustaining a commitment to public service. A national group of educators and police officials, assembled as an advisory council for the International Association of Chiefs of Police under a Ford Foundation grant, put their case this way:

> Generally, it is conceded that today's law enforcement officer has a need for higher education. It is also generally agreed that within the next few years law enforcement officers will find higher education imperative.
>
> The above observation is the result of consideration of the changes that society has and is experiencing in such areas as the population explosion, the growing pressure for education beyond high school, the changing nature of metropolitan areas, and the effects of tensions and pressures ranging from automation to race. The law enforcement officer is required to meet all kinds of people and innumerable kinds of situations; he must therefore: (1) be equipped to make good value judgments (2) be able to maintain his perspective (3) be able to understand the underlying causes of human behavior (4) be able to communicate clearly and precisely (5) possess leadership qualities (6) be knowledgeable of skills. In view of changing conditions which require flexibility, basic theory, and broad understandings, it is concluded that a wide spectrum of higher education must be available.[8]

Accordingly, the IACP leadership has argued with increasing vigor in recent years that

> ... the campus must be looked to for the police officers of the future. It is nonsense to state or to assume that the enforcement of the law is so simple a task that it can be done best by those unencumbered by an inquiring mind nurtured by a study of the liberal arts. The man who goes into our streets in hopes of regulating, directing or controlling human behavior must be armed with more than a gun and the ability to perform mechanical movements in response to a situation. Such men as these engage in the difficult, complex and important business of human behavior. Their intel-

8. Statement by the IACP Advisory Committee (processed, 1965).

lectual armament—so long restricted to the minimum—must be no less than their physical prowess and protection.[9]

The International Association of Police Professors, an association of professionals in two-year and four-year institutions, has also made an explicit statement of the need for a liberal arts education:

> One can justify requiring art, music, literature, on the grounds that a policeman, in his work, sees so much of the seamy side of humanity that he should have some acquaintance with the sublime and noble products of the human spirit in order to keep his sanity, balance, and judgment. But these are not the real justifications; rather, we justify the requirements of liberal arts in law enforcement education on the grounds that they contribute in ways for which no substitute has been found, to the development of men as thinking, critical, creative beings, with an awareness of their relations to the whole of mankind. We do this in the faith that this type of man is a better man—whatever occupation he pursues.[10]

Such arguments have been stated and restated since August Vollmer formulated the proposition half a century ago. Yet the need for general collegiate education for police has only recently begun to win acceptance. In 1968, according to an IACP study, less than 12 percent of 427 reporting departments provided preferential pay incentives for credits toward college degrees.[11] The belief persists that higher education is not necessary for routine police tasks and that recruitment of college-educated policemen is not worth the effort because such "overly qualified" men will soon become dissatisfied and leave the service. Until recent years, the suspicion that a little education for police might be a dangerous thing has typified the attitude of local officials. A publication of the International City Managers' Association in the 1950s held

9. Quinn Tamm, editorial in *Police Chief*, Vol. 32 (May 1965), p. 6.
10. "Report of the Committee To Establish Guidelines for the Development of Law Enforcement Programs" (processed, 1966). The association, founded in 1962, has about one hundred members. It maintains no staff and has no means of promulgating or enforcing the actions taken by its committee.
11. Unpublished 1968 training survey. The percentage for all departments is probably lower, since smaller departments, which usually have lower educational standards, were underrepresented in the responses received.

that advanced schooling "is not essential" and that to recruit men of higher intelligence "is inviting trouble. A relatively small percentage of policemen will receive promotions. The rest must be content to remain policemen. The higher the I.Q., generally speaking, the more ambitious, and, therefore the more frustrated and disaffected. . . ." In the 1961 edition of this publication, however, the ICMA reversed its position, declaring that the complexities of modern law enforcement require that "the police recruit must be above average intelligence" and approving the trend toward higher educational requirements.[12]

Enlightened public administration doctrine has long held that entrants in a career service should be selected with a view to promotion to the level they may ultimately be expected to reach. Educational requirements should therefore not be based solely on the duties of the lower positions, although in the case of the police service intelligence and education are as necessary for competent performance at the entry level as in the executive ranks. Beyond technical skills and vocational training, the patrolman's job requires

> a vast reservoir of knowledge in order to be able to know when and how to perform his duties. To be fully capable, the police student must be educated in terms of the total man. The officer must know much more than the contents of the Criminal Code and when a "criminal offense has in fact been committed"; he must know his position in the total framework of society, the rights as well as the obligations of the citizenry, and the dignity of man.[13]

There is, however, evidence to support the claim that better-educated and more intelligent men are more liable to experience frustration and dissatisfaction within the police system and ultimately leave its ranks.[14] Some police administrators deny this is a

12. *Municipal Police Administration* (International City Managers' Association, 1954), p. 146; (1961), p. 131.
13. Thomas M. Frost, *A Forward Look in Police Education* (Charles C Thomas, 1959), p. 34.
14. One large sample established a negative relationship between higher educational levels and retention on the force (Ruth Levy, "Summary of Report on Retrospective Study of 5,000 Peace Officer Personnel Records," *Police Yearbook*, 1966 [IACP], p. 62). The study drew the conclusion that police departments "do

problem, maintaining that "the superior quality of service provided by the more intelligent policeman justifies a higher turnover" and that they would rather have in their departments "one
good man for one year than a bum for twenty years." [15] In any case,
the fact that college-educated men may become dissatisfied with
the service is not a sufficient argument against their recruitment.
It is, rather, an argument for reform of the system to provide
greater incentives and more opportunities for qualified men. Such
steps toward higher levels of professionalism should also provide
the basis for a long-run solution to the problem of retention. The
tensions that arose in the interim between noncollege members of
the force and a favored minority with a college education could
be reduced by offering incentives to all officers to extend their
education. Education would thus become not the measure of a
good policeman but a means to make good ones better.

There have been other challenges to the premise that better-
educated men make better policemen. Local officials in some
communities have opposed salary increases for police with credits
toward a college degree on the basis of a single limited study
which reported that the productivity of patrolmen in one city
declined as their years of college increased. The study rated patrolmen quantitatively on routine tasks (numbers of parking tickets
issued, vehicles stopped, pedestrians questioned, and so on), not
qualitatively. It did not measure performance of the peacekeeping
function, which consumes most of a policeman's time, or such
critical factors as individual judgment and capacity to handle

---

not sufficiently meet the needs of their better educated officers." Arthur Neiderhoffer, in *Behind the Shield: The Police in Urban Society* (Doubleday, 1967),
makes the point that men with higher levels of education tend to become more
frustrated and cynical the longer they remain patrolmen because their expectations
are higher (p. 235). In an unpublished IACP survey of 4,672 experienced policemen in 1968, Nelson A. Watson found that little thought had been given to leaving
the service by 86 percent of those who had not completed high school, 79 percent
of high-school graduates, 74 percent of those with some college courses, and 67
percent of those with degrees.

15. First comment by O. W. Wilson, in *Police Administration* (2d ed.;
McGraw-Hill, 1963), p. 145; second quoted by Gene S. Muehleisen in "Mandatory
Minimums or Professional Maximums," *Police Yearbook, 1965*, p. 315.

unexpected situations. (Even on the basis of mechanical performance, however, patrolmen with thirteen years of education stood highest in the composite ranking.) The author was careful not to generalize from his findings, cautioning that "more or less formal education did not, *per se*, mean that more or less police work was accomplished by the patrolmen in the sample population" [16]—a lack of correlation that undoubtedly obtains in other occupations as well.

Achievement of more meaningful research is handicapped by the relatively small number of college graduates serving in police ranks. Most departments have had little experience with college graduates, and some chiefs have undoubtedly formed their impressions from the performance of a few marginal products of marginal institutions. In California, New York City, and other cities where significant numbers of college graduates have been recruited, police administrators are impressed with their performance and outspoken in advocacy of more such recruits:

> ... When all other factors are equal the university-trained man is better qualified for police service than one who has graduated only from high school. He has had broader experience with people and new situations; his adaptability has been tested; he has had the opportunity to meet students of many different nationalities, cultural backgrounds, and racial characteristics.... His studies will have given him a new perspective on the problems and aspirations common to all men, and he will have learned to some degree to withhold judgment and to restrain his actions and impulses in favor of calm consideration and analysis.[17]

Those who have progressed through a college program have demonstrated a competitive ability far superior to those who come to us with a general education development certificate.[18]

16. Thomas J. McGreevy, "A Field Study of the Relationship between the Formal Education Levels of 556 Police Officers in St. Louis, Missouri, and Their Patrol Duty Performance Records" (master's thesis, School of Public Administration and Public Safety, Michigan State University, 1964; on file in IACP Center for Law Enforcement Research Information), p. 61.
17. Wilson, *Police Administration*, p. 139.
18. Bernard L. Garmire, "Personnel Leadership Development," *Police Year-book, 1964*, p. 333.

Candidates with a minimum of two years of college are easier to train on the complexities of changes in the rules of evidence, search and seizure, arrest and court techniques. They are more susceptible to training on specialty items, such as internal and external intelligence, public relations, budgeting and auxiliary services, they are more adept at adjusting to situations that require clear thinking and precise action.[19]

Some of the departments which have actively sought college-educated officers report that they score markedly higher on efficiency ratings by their superiors. In Flint, Michigan, a random sample of 19 officers with at least 60 hours of college credit averaged 85.22 on performance ratings over a six-month period, compared with a 76.35 average for a similar number of officers without college education.[20] A university research team analyzing the performance patterns of 500 Chicago patrolmen found that the highest-rated group of long-tenured officers had significantly higher educational achievement than other groups and had demonstrated a continuing interest in technical or professional development after completion of their academic studies.[21]

There is some evidence that college-educated police differ from their colleagues in personality characteristics and attitudes toward the law enforcement task. One study has reported "highly significant differences" between the two groups:

... Police who are attracted to college are significantly less authoritarian than police who are not impelled to attend college. This implies that there are certain personality characteristics of police who attend college that make it more likely that they will be able to function more effectively with respect to the problem stemming from civil rights demonstrations and more effectively in accordance

19. William H. Berlin, Jr., chief of the Hermosa Beach, Calif., Police Department, quoted in Donald E. Clark and Samuel G. Chapman, *A Forward Step: Educational Backgrounds for Police* (Charles C Thomas, 1966), p. 84.
20. James W. Rutherford, chief of police of Flint, Mich., in a letter to the author, Feb. 27, 1968.
21. Melany E. Baehr, John E. Furcon, and Ernest C. Froemel, "Psychological Assessment of Patrolman Qualifications in Relation to Field Performance," Preliminary Report to Office of Law Enforcement Assistance, Department of Justice (processed, 1968).

with the guidelines set down by the Supreme Court with respect to arrests and search and seizure.[22]

A national sample of 4,672 policemen has revealed some interesting differences between college and noncollege officers in the perception of their role and in approaches to the concepts of justice and law. For example, the lower the educational level, the greater the tendency to view the law as fixed and inflexible.[23] The statement that "as long as a law is on the books the police must enforce it" was supported by 71 percent of policemen who were not high-school graduates, 67 percent of high-school graduates without any college credit, 59 percent of those with some college education, and 53 percent of those with college degrees. Such findings are not conclusive, but they suggest that large-scale recruitment of college graduates would significantly affect police performance.

The most compelling argument for higher educational standards for police is the steadily rising educational level of the general population. In 1946, only 22 percent of all persons between 18 and 21 were enrolled in institutions of higher education; in 1967 the figure was 46.6 percent. The trend is continuing: 58.7 percent of all males who graduated from high school in the spring of 1966 enrolled in college that fall.[24] National manpower policies are accelerating the trend, encouraging college attendance through federal support of loans, fellowships, and work-study programs, as well as draft deferments and other special incentives in fields designated as critically important to the national interest

22. Alexander B. Smith, Bernard Locke, and William F. Walker, "Authoritarianism in College and Non-College Oriented Police," *Journal of Criminal Law, Criminology, and Police Science,* Vol. 58 (March 1967), p. 132.

23. Unpublished study for IACP by Nelson A. Watson, 1968. "Such a view of the law can create difficulties because it predisposes police to seek out quasi-legal or illegal solutions to their perceived problems" (John H. McNamara, "Uncertainties in Police Work: Recruits' Backgrounds and Training," in *The Police: Six Sociological Essays,* ed. David J. Bordua [John Wiley and Sons, 1967], p. 250). Such a view also tends to deny the role of discretion in police work. See discussion in Chapter 2, pp. 23–25.

24. U.S. Office of Education, *Digest of Educational Statistics, 1968* (Government Printing Office, 1968), pp. 68, 116.

(health, science, teaching, urban planning). More rapid acceleration is likely in the years ahead. A growing list of educational and governmental leaders have expressed support for extending public education beyond high school. The National Commission on Technology, Automation, and Economic Progress in 1966 recommended establishment of a nationwide system of "free public education through 2 years beyond high school" that would be available to all Americans, with vocational and occupational training functions shifted from the high school to the post-secondary level.[25] Similar proposals have been made by other public and private study commissions. The Carnegie Commission on Higher Education has called for removal of financial barriers for all youth who enroll in academic or occupational programs as "one of the most urgent national priorities for higher education."[26]

These trends have already raised the educational attainment of large portions of the population significantly beyond that of the police. The median years of school completed by employed males in the civilian labor force is 16.3 for professional and technical workers, 12.7 for managers, officials, and proprietors, 12.8 for sales workers, and 12.5 for clerical workers, as compared with 12.4 for police.[27] The Bureau of the Census estimates that in 1970 the median years of school completed by persons 25–29 years of age will reach 12.5, and by all persons over 25 years of age, 12.1.[28]

As educational attainment rises, so do entry standards in other occupations, intensifying competition for the talented manpower which is so desperately needed in law enforcement. The 1967

25. National Commission on Technology, Automation, and Economic Progress, *Technology and the American Economy* (Government Printing Office, 1966), p. 46.
26. Carnegie Commission on Higher Education, *Quality and Equality: New Levels of Federal Responsibility for Higher Education* (McGraw-Hill, 1968), p. 17.
27. U.S. Office of Education, *Digest of Educational Statistics, 1968*, p. 117. The estimate for police is for 1966, reported in U.S. President's Commission on Law Enforcement and Administration of Justice, *Task Force Report: The Police* (Government Printing Office, 1967), p. 10.
28. U.S. Bureau of the Census, *Current Population Reports: Population Estimates*, Series P-25, No. 390, March 29, 1968.

Manpower Report of the President noted that employment requirements arc rising most rapidly in the professional, service, clerical, managerial, skilled, and sales categories and that occupations in these categories have the highest percentages of workers who learned their jobs through formal training. These occupations also have higher levels of educational attainment than other occupational groups: "Indeed, in each of the rapidly growing white-collar fields, the average worker, in 1966, had received some education beyond high school." [29] The growing tendency of employers to require higher levels of education in response to the increasing availability of educated workers is reflected in the course offerings which are now common in two-year institutions. For example, the 1968–69 directory of Chicago City College lists two-year career programs in hotel management, insurance, merchandising, real estate, office occupations, air conditioning, motor transportation, paint technology, recreation (for aides), teaching (for aides), and ornamental horticulture, among others.

For the police service, therefore, a time of decision is at hand. It cannot attract more qualified personnel unless an effort is mounted, on a state, regional, and national basis, to approach the educational standard recommended by the President's Commission on Law Enforcement. And the commission warned that "it never will be implemented if a strong movement toward it does not begin at once." [30] In fact, an ambitious effort to raise educational standards will be necessary just to maintain the status quo, with all its attendant problems of personnel quality and quantity. Failure to overtake or at least keep pace with rising standards in other occupations will mean that recruits will have to be drawn increasingly from the minority of the population least educated, least talented, and least qualified to assume the responsibilities of modern law enforcement. Such a trend is already observable

29. *Manpower Report of the President and a Report on Manpower Requirements, Resources, Utilization, and Training by the United States Department of Labor, 1967* (Government Printing Office, 1967), p. 159.
30. U.S. President's Commission on Law Enforcement, *The Challenge of Crime in a Free Society*, p. 110.

to some authorities: "There is no question in the minds of most law enforcement officials that the quality of manpower entering the field—especially the police—has been going down over the last twenty years." [31]

To debate the value of higher education for police, then, is largely irrelevant. In other occupations involving lesser demands, a general liberal-arts education is expected as a background for specialized training. The real question is not, "Do police need a college degree?" but, "Where are persons with the necessary qualifications to be found?" More and more, the search leads directly to the college and university campus. As for inservice officers, the question is not whether those without higher education are unqualified but whether advanced study would make them better policemen.

What Kinds of Programs for Police?

There is no common agreement among police officials or educators as to what is meant by "higher education for police," and the resultant confusion further complicates efforts to raise professional standards or to develop new educational programs. Several different kinds and levels of college programs already exist as sources of potential recruits or as the means of upgrading existing personnel.

At the junior-college level there are general education programs leading to an associate degree, several distinct varieties of law enforcement degree programs ranging in emphasis from technical skills to liberal arts, work experience programs combining classroom work with on-the-job training, and one-year certificate programs which are heavily vocation-oriented. Institutions may also conduct a variety of short-term, noncredit courses and institutes, as well as campus-based training programs.

31. James Q. Wilson, "A Reader's Guide to the Crime Commission Reports," *Public Interest*, Fall 1967, p. 81.

At the four-year college level, degree programs across the full range of the liberal arts and the sciences are potential sources of recruits, in addition to the baccalaureate programs in police science. There are also a small number of graduate programs leading to masters and doctoral degrees in law enforcement, criminal justice, and police administration. It is important to distinguish between the various programs, and to identify their strengths and weaknesses.

JUNIOR-COLLEGE LEVEL

The two-year public community colleges are unique in their three-part mission to offer *transfer programs* for students who may pursue higher academic studies, *occupational programs* to meet local and regional needs for development of skilled manpower, and *public service programs* to provide opportunities for retraining and development of existing manpower in the community. Because they seek to meet the various needs of such a wide spectrum of ages, interests, and abilities, these institutions have become the fastest-growing sector of higher education in the last decade. Two-year campuses already exist in every state, and between 50 and 60 new ones are being opened each year. At this rate, low-cost post–high school education will be accessible to all citizens within another decade. In any national plans to upgrade police manpower at both entry and inservice levels, the two-year colleges will play a central role.

General Education. There were over 1,700,000 students enrolled in some 950 nonprofit junior and community colleges in the United States in the fall of 1968. Approximately 24,000 of them in 199 institutions were enrolled in law enforcement programs; the rest constitute a virtually untapped source of manpower for the police service. Few local police agencies recruit from this large population group; fewer agencies encourage their personnel to enroll in institutions which do not offer a police curriculum. Yet specialists maintain that courses available in any junior college are a useful background for law enforcement:

Courses, such as English, sociology, psychology, political science, logic, and history are the very foundation of law enforcement's body of knowledge. . . . Any community college in operation today can offer a year's course in English composition. Likewise, it can expose the individual to the organized study of society and human behavior, along with social problem analysis. In addition, courses are available in general psychology, mental health, understanding group interaction, and personality development. . . . Courses in logic and the physical sciences will help to equip the law enforcement student with an awareness of fact recognition and to enhance his scientific deductive talents. . . . Any college offering freshman and sophomore level courses can effectively serve as a starting point for the education of police personnel.[32]

The desirability of higher education for police is not diminished by the unavailability of a formal degree program in law enforcement. Limitations of geography, staffing, and funding make it practically impossible to bring specialized courses within reach of every police agency in the near future. Therefore the general education programs in the area should receive major attention in any short-range strategy to upgrade police personnel. The police service must come to recognize the value of a general academic program by establishing recruiting beachheads on the junior-college campuses and by providing salary incentives for inservice personnel to earn credits in general education courses as well as in specialized professional programs.

Law Enforcement Degree Programs. Associate degree programs in law enforcement were offered by 199 community colleges in 37 states, the District of Columbia, Guam, and the Virgin Islands in the fall of 1968. These programs originated shortly after the Second World War in the junior-college system of California, enabling that state to make police education and training available to virtually all its local police agencies within a decade. The pat-

32. Thompson S. Crockett and James D. Stinchcomb, *Guidelines for Law Enforcement Education Programs in Community and Junior Colleges* (American Association of Junior Colleges, 1968), p. 16.

tern has been widely copied in recent years: whereas only 8 programs existed in other states in 1960, 141 institutions in 36 other states offered associate degree programs in the fall of 1968. Total enrollment has grown from 9,000 to 24,000 in the same period.

Although the upward trend in police programs is continuing, their availability is still far from universal. Five states account for over half of the programs; 13 states have none; another 10 have 1 each. Two-year degree programs are unavailable to police in most of New England, the central plains states, and the mountain states and in large portions of the South.[33] Statewide availability is as yet a reality only in California.

Among institutions there is wide variation in law enforcement programs, reflecting different program objectives and a lack of consensus on the nature and purpose of higher education for police. Three distinct types of curriculum patterns can be identified:

1. An occupational program emphasizing skills required by the local police department, designed for students who intend to enter the force upon completion of their course of study.

2. A transfer program emphasizing liberal arts subjects, designed for preservice or inservice students who plan to continue their education and wish to meet lower division credit requirements.

3. A balanced program, including a basic core of background professional courses and general education offerings selected for their relevance to law enforcement, designed to meet the needs of both terminal and transfer students.

Whatever the curriculum pattern, law enforcement programs attempt to provide a sound professional orientation through a sequence of specialized courses acquainting the student with the historical and philosophical basis for the police service, its role in the total structure of government, and a related body of knowledge concerning the American system of justice, criminal law, rules of evidence, the theory of criminal behavior, and concepts of police organization and management. Much of this theoretical

33. *Law Enforcement Education Directory, 1968–69* [International Association of Chiefs of Police]. States without any two-year police programs are Arkansas, Louisiana, Maine, Minnesota, Mississippi, Montana, New Hampshire, North Dakota, Oklahoma, South Carolina, South Dakota, Vermont, and West Virginia.

background may be acquired in a general education program, but it is largely absent from police training, which necessarily emphasizes the practical procedures and techniques.

Work Experience Programs. A promising new variant in police education is the cooperative education program in which police cadets are recruited from high school, employed in a variety of duties and given basic training in police agencies, and required to complete a two-year college degree program before acceptance as sworn members of the force. Such programs pose some difficult problems of supervision and responsibility (for example, security clearance of students for part-time work and liability for them in dangerous situations) which have not been fully resolved between police agencies and academic institutions. For these reasons, the training value and economic feasibility of cooperative work experience programs have not been widely accepted by police agencies. Only about twenty departments currently sponsor them. Nevertheless, some authorities are convinced that work experience programs have a large potential for recruiting capable young people before they become committed to other occupations. Such programs also provide longer, more effective probationary periods, more systematic training, and a more comprehensive theoretical background for recruits, while releasing regular personnel for other important police functions.[34]

One-Year Certificate Programs. Since these programs are designed primarily to fill a vocational rather than an educational function, they might be classified more accurately as training programs. Like the short-term courses, seminars, and institutes which colleges are increasingly conducting in cooperation with local police departments, they are usually designed to meet specific training objectives for inservice personnel. Unlike the shorter courses, however, certificate programs are fully applicable toward an associate degree, offering half of the required number of credits.

34. See Jimmie C. Styles and Denny F. Pace, *Guidelines for Work Experience Programs in the Criminal Justice System* (American Association of Junior Colleges, 1969).

To this extent they may be useful in encouraging policemen who would otherwise be unlikely to pursue their education to return to school. They are often transitional programs, offered while a two-year law enforcement curriculum is being developed. After the curriculum is established, most certificate programs are phased out. In 1968 only six institutions, all without two-year degree programs, reported offering certificate programs.

BACCALAUREATE PROGRAMS

General Education. The advantages of a general education for police, noted above for the two-year institutions, are equally valid at the four-year level. Any effort to attract better-qualified candidates to the police service must take account of the largest potential source of talented manpower: the baccalaureate programs which enroll about 5.5 million students and annually confer some 500,000 degrees in colleges and universities in every state of the union. This pool of talent is expanding rapidly: by 1975, four-year enrollments are projected at 7.4 million.

As the President's Commission Task Force on Police observed, there is no inherent reason why the challenges of modern law enforcement should not offer stimulating career opportunities for able college graduates. Moreover, as recognition grows that administration of an urban police department requires highly skilled specialists, the potential recruitment base should be broadened beyond the four-year liberal arts schools to the graduate schools of business, law, engineering, and other professional, scientific, and technical fields.

This pool cannot be tapped in substantial numbers, however, unless improvements are made in salary and working conditions, together with an overhaul of the entire police personnel system along the lines recommended by the President's Commission on Law Enforcement. Students pursuing the general education curriculums of the nation's colleges and universities are at best only a long-range source of personnel. But plans to tap this source should be built into the development of manpower policies that will enhance careers in law enforcement.

Law Enforcement Degree Programs. Baccalaureate programs in law enforcement, which originated in California under the leadership of August Vollmer in the 1930s, grew slowly until the early 1960s. Between 1963 and 1968 they doubled in number, apparently in response to the growing pressure from two-year institutions for transfer programs. By 1968 they enrolled 8,378 undergraduate and graduate students in 44 institutions scattered through every region of the country. Over half of this group are inservice personnel, suggesting that they increasingly recognize the importance of education.[35] On the other hand, over half of the preservice graduates fail to enter law enforcement—a statistic which reflects the low status of the profession even among those with a demonstrated interest, and the difficulties of opening up this potentially significant source of police manpower.

Masters programs in law enforcement are offered by 13 institutions in 7 states; 5 of these institutions in 3 states also offer Ph.D. programs. California alone accounts for almost half of the graduate programs. Their enrollment is small, and they have as yet had little effect in attracting qualified persons into local departments: most of their graduates enter federal, military, retail, and industrial security agencies instead. Nevertheless the graduate programs have important potential for developing an elite vanguard in the movement toward higher standards of professionalization. Their numbers may swell significantly as federal funds become more widely available for police education.

FEDERAL ASSISTANCE

Federal assistance for police education was established under the Law Enforcement Assistance Act of 1965. It may be, in fact, that the act's greatest contribution was in the field of education,

35. Charles L. Newman and Dorothy Sue Hunter, "Education for Careers in Law Enforcement," *Journal of Criminal Law, Criminology, and Police Science* Vol. 59 (March 1968), pp. 139–40.

although the word itself does not appear in the legislation. In the three years of LEAA's existence, some fifty grants were awarded to establish college degree programs in police science. These were a major factor in the rapid expansion of two-year police degree programs which occurred during the period.

The 1968 omnibus bill which superseded the 1965 law authorized further programs of academic assistance. Loans up to $1,800 a year were provided for persons enrolled in approved full-time undergraduate or graduate degree programs. Police and correctional personnel of states and local agencies were given priority for the loans, which are forgivable at the rate of 25 percent for each complete year of subsequent service in a law enforcement agency. Grants were also authorized to pay tuition and fees up to $200 per academic quarter or $300 per semester for inservice officers enrolled on a full-time or part-time basis in approved undergraduate or graduate programs. Tuition grant recipients had to agree to remain in law enforcement for two years following completion of their studies. Expenditures for these programs totaled $3.2 million in 1969, and were estimated at over $18 million for 1970.

Although the academic assistance provisions of the 1968 act may prove to be among its greatest long-range benefits, some immediate problems are evident. Grants and loans will stimulate development of additional collegiate programs, but do not provide a means of improving their quality or their relevance for local police agencies. The act does nothing to promote the establishment of educational standards for degree programs or their common acceptance by the colleges and the police service.

More inservice personnel will undoubtedly take advantage of the loans and tuition grants to advance their own education, but no incentives are provided for local departments to actively encourage the participation of their own men. Such incentives are needed, for many departments actually discourage part-time study by refusing to take account of educational attainment in promotion procedures and salary schedules, and by reluctance to permit the schedule shifts which may be necessary for individuals to attend academic courses.

More preservice students may be induced to enter local police agencies for the four years required to obtain forgiveness of their loans, but there is little reason to believe that they will necessarily remain in the service in larger proportions than at present as long as salaries and working conditions in federal investigative agencies or related private employment are more attractive.

Although qualified instructors are already in short supply in college degree programs, the law provides no means of increasing their numbers; rather, it may actually contribute to the shortage by increasing the number of students, and intensify the deficiencies which are already apparent in the quality of instruction.

In summary, two primary weaknesses are apparent in the educational assistance provided by the 1968 act. It does little to strengthen the quality of collegiate programs in law enforcement. Nor does it relate these programs closely enough to the act's training provisions to assure that, once policemen receive an appropriate educational background, they will continue to receive the training they need to make the most of it. Perhaps more important than these weaknesses is the law's failure to encourage those reforms of the police service that would make careers in law enforcement increasingly attractive to college-educated personnel.

How Good Are College Law Enforcement Programs?

The growth of college programs for police has been so recent and so rapid that the implications for the profession are not yet entirely clear. What is apparent is that programs at all levels have not reached their full potential, and that their role in higher education is not yet clearly defined.

The appearance of a "police curriculum" has generated controversy and considerable confusion in the academic world. In the community colleges, where growth has been most marked, there is no consensus on the proper educational mix; courses offered for degree credits range from literature and philosophy to traffic control and marksmanship. Most programs are still too new for meaningful evaluation, and as yet there is no agency recognized as competent to perform this task. In the four-year institutions, police programs must cope with suspicions that the field is not sufficiently defined as a discipline to merit full academic respectability. (A more important obstacle may be the growing radicalization of the American college campus, which has added the contempt of student militants for the police and all authority figures to the natural antipathy between the liberal academic community and the police as protectors of middle-class ideological values.)

Similar uncertainties characterize the police community. The IACP's strong support for higher education, through its official pronouncements and its staff studies, is undoubtedly ahead of its membership. The nation's police chiefs are far from unanimous in their attitudes: some call explicitly for a general collegiate education; some argue for extended technical education which they tend to equate with campus-based training; others are doubtful, indifferent, or scornful of the whole idea of sending policemen to college or seeking recruits on the campus.

The lack of consensus among educators and police as to the nature and objectives of law enforcement programs raises questions about their value and effectiveness. The President's Commission Task Force on Police noted that "there has been far too little analysis either by the police or by the colleges and universities of their educational needs." [36] Careful evaluation of existing programs is needed before criteria can be established for judging their adequacy. Unless such steps are taken, the continued growth of police degree programs may create an educational monstrosity.

PROBLEM AREAS

Community college police programs are an educational no-man's-land, without recognized standards for course offerings or

36. U.S. President's Commission on Law Enforcement, *Task Force Report: The Police*, p. 128.

their content, quality of instruction, or awarding of credit. The first attempt to provide guidance for the development of quality programs was made by the American Association of Junior Colleges in 1968 with the publication of its *Guidelines for Law Enforcement Education Programs in Community and Junior Colleges.* The authors recommended adoption of a balanced program of general education and professional courses as the best way "to meet the current and future needs of the police profession" and outlined a specific curriculum:

FIRST YEAR

First Term	Credit hours	Second Term	Credit hours
English	3	English	3
Psychology, Introduction	3	National Government	3
State and Local		Sociology, Introduction	3
Government	3	Police Operations	3
Introduction to Law		Police Role in Crime and	
Enforcement	3	Delinquency	3
Police Administration	3	Physical Education	1
Physical Education	1		

SECOND YEAR

Third Term	Credit hours	Fourth Term	Credit hours
Humanities	3	Adolescent Psychology or	
Criminal Law	3	Social Problems	3
Mathematics	3	Logic	3
Criminal Investigation	3	Criminal Evidence and	
Public Speaking	3	Procedure	3
Physical Education	1	Introduction to	
		Criminalistics	3
		Elective	3
		Physical Education	1

The authors of the AAJC pamphlet also made detailed suggestions for the content of the professional courses:

Introduction to Law Enforcement
History, development, and philosophy of law enforcement in democratic society; introduction to agencies involved in the administration of criminal justice; career orientation.

Police Administration
Principles of organization and management as applied to law enforcement agencies; introduction to concepts of organizational behavior.

Police Operations
Line activities of law enforcement agencies with emphasis on the patrol function and the prevention of crime; includes traffic, investigative, juvenile, vice, and other specialized operational units.

Police Role in Crime and Delinquency
Introduction to deviant behavior and current criminological theories with emphasis on synthesis and police applications; crime prevention and the phenomena of crime.

Criminal Law
Local, state, and federal laws; their development, application, and enforcement.

Criminal Evidence and Procedure
Criminal evidence for police, types of evidence; criminal procedure in various courts; arrest, search, and seizure, collection of evidence, discretion, and related topics.

Criminal Investigation
Fundamentals of criminal investigation; theory and history; crime scene to courtroom with emphasis on techniques appropriate to specific crimes.

Introduction to Criminalistics
Physical evidence, collection, identification, preservation, and transportation; crime laboratory capability and limitations; examination of physical evidence within resources of the investigator and demonstration of laboratory criminalistics to the extent supported by existing or available facilities.[37]

37. Crockett and Stinchcomb, *Guidelines for Law Enforcement Education Programs in Community and Junior Colleges*, pp. 18–19. The AAJC also suggested the content for electives (traffic, police auxiliary services, community relations, and supervision) and physical education options (defense tactics, firearms, first aid).

Publication of guidelines, however, is not a substitute for the adoption of recognized standards within the field. To date, no mechanism exists for the development of such standards or for assuring their enforcement. Consequently, there is no way to assess the strengths and weaknesses of community college programs in general. Each program is a product of the unique interrelationships between the community, its academic institution, and its law enforcement agency.

Wherever programs are compared, wide variations may be found. The most striking variation from one campus to another is the extent to which technical police subjects are emphasized:

> The Commission's examination of these programs disclosed that many of them are highly vocational in nature and are primarily intended to provide technical skills necessary in performing police work. College credit is given, for example, for such courses as traffic control, defensive tactics and patrol procedures. Although there is a need for vocational training, it is not and cannot be a substitute for a liberal arts education. . . . The wisdom of giving degree credit for technical courses, therefore, must be questioned.[38]

Police subjects comprise more than two-thirds of the credits required for a police degree in some two-year institutions. Others with a strong liberal arts orientation may require less than one-third of degree credits to be in police subjects. Programs supported by state vocational education departments must meet rigid requirements which in effect mandate an overemphasis on technical skills. And no matter how well these skills are taught, their preponderance in the curriculum necessarily limits the student's exposure to the values of the humanities and the communication arts, the rigors of mathematics, logic, and the sciences, and the broad body of knowledge—including law, government, and the social sciences—that provides a sound professional orientation. Many programs do not explore this body of knowledge very deeply, others hardly at all. One college lists only two required general education courses: English Composition and Technical

38. U.S. President's Commission on Law Enforcement, *Task Force Report: The Police*, p. 127.

English. Others clutter their list of required subjects with such courses as firearms, first aid, and judo. Police drill, report writing, typing, and water safety are among the credit courses commonly found in the IACP's *Law Enforcement Education Directory, 1968–69.* The equation of remedial offerings with general education subjects and the substitution of vocational skills for the academic disciplines typify the confusion over the content of police education.

Further confusion is evident in the course sequence of some programs. A curriculum which offers Administration of Justice in the fourth quarter instead of presenting it as an introductory course, or which offers American Government simultaneously with Criminal Law instead of presenting the former as a prerequisite for the latter reveals a lack of attention to continuity and cumulative curriculum development.

A few colleges permit the substitution of prior work experience or attendance at police training academies for degree credit. This practice may attract inservice students, but it would be unthinkable in a strong educational institution, since students attracted by substitute-credit arrangements would be likely to experience difficulties in the later years of a degree program if they decided to continue their education.[39] University faculties do not grant transfer credits lightly, and graduates of two-year programs sometimes find that much of their earlier work is not acceptable toward a bachelor's degree. Such problems of articulation with the four-year institutions are likely to persist, due to the vocational emphasis of so many two-year programs.

On the other hand, such problems of articulation are not sufficient cause to question the validity of career-oriented programs. Until such time as the four-year degree standard becomes a reality

39. One community college almost made it possible to work one's way through college without actually matriculating, offering up to 45 credits of a 60-credit degree program for service in the local police department (rank has its privileges: captains were allowed more credits than sergeants, and sergeants more than patrolmen). After a consultant pointed out that this based educational achievement on advancement in the ranks rather than vice versa, the program was modified.

for police throughout the nation, as proposed by the President's Commission on Law Enforcement, there is no reason why two-year programs must necessarily be fully transferable. As long as the police service generally does not require higher education in any form, programs with a preponderance of vocational content fill a real need in view of the evident limitations of training in most local agencies. Transferability of credits may become essential for two-year degree programs in the future, as educational requirements rise. For the present, however, it is not as important as provision of quality programs whatever their orientation. An interim solution might be the development of a double-track system, in which the more highly qualified students would be counseled to follow a course of study which would be fully transferable toward a four-year degree.

Some curriculum deficiencies are attributable to the limitations of the faculty. Persons with both the academic qualifications and the professional experience to teach law enforcement subjects are in short supply, and police programs in two-year institutions tend to be one-man departments, supplemented by lecturers from local criminal justice agencies. The IACP's 1968 survey of law enforcement education found 189 full-time faculty for 151 reporting institutions. Only about half of them held graduate degrees, although almost all had previous experience in law enforcement. Of 918 part-time faculty, only 29 percent held advanced degrees. Faculty for the 42 baccalaureate programs reporting totaled 178, 87 percent of them with advanced degrees and 33 percent without law enforcement experience (47 percent with less than five years' experience).

Such statistics suggest the difficulties involved in providing qualified instruction across the entire spectrum of the law enforcement curriculum. The teacher with professional background in the behavioral sciences may have little familiarity with the subject of crime investigation, while the instructor with police experience may have little command of the psychology of deviant behavior or background in law enforcement theory. As in other academic departments, the curriculum is likely to develop along the lines of faculty specialties, and the smaller the department, the greater the likelihood that teaching will be weak in important subject areas. The greater the emphasis on vocational courses, the less the likelihood that qualified instruction will be provided in broader areas of academic learning. Academically oriented programs, on the other hand, may more easily overcome their weaknesses by drawing heavily on qualified instructors from other departments.

Students as well as faculty influence the strengths and weaknesses of the curriculum. Most full-time students are recent high-school graduates, uncertain of their future careers, whereas part-time students are generally inservice policemen. The proportion of each has obvious effects on the type of program offered. Where inservice students predominate, there is a tendency for two-year degree programs to emphasize skill courses and to proliferate specialties of particular interest to the local police departments. Discipline problems on the force may inspire a course in Supervision; a growing drug problem in the community may bring a course in Narcotics. Such subjects may justifiably have a place as units in broader courses on personnel administration or problems of social control and behavior, but their development into credit offerings reduces the time available for conveying the body of knowledge that lower division courses should provide. Too many specialized or vocational courses may also cause full-time students to lose interest in a police career. On the other hand, an academic program without sufficient grounding in the realities of law enforcement may be unacceptable to inservice personnel.

Institutions face other problems in accommodating the needs of both full-time and part-time students. Their combination in the same class may accentuate the inadequacies of teachers with limited experience. Other burdens are placed on the faculty by the need of inservice students for close liaison with local law enforcement officials and more flexible scheduling of classes. Full-time students have another distinct set of needs and problems.

Many institutions fail to provide them with adequate counseling; as a result there is a high dropout rate of preservice students and thus a loss of potentially good police officers. Variations in selection requirements may make effective counseling difficult; some programs deny admission to students unless they meet the physical standards of the local police agency, even though standards are not uniform for the country as a whole or for the wide range of careers opening up in the field of criminal justice. Other difficulties are created by the poor image of the police in the community and the tendency of high-school counselors to direct "nonacademic" students into law enforcement.[40]

Such difficulties are certain to increase, for enrollment of both full-time and part-time students in two-year programs is growing rapidly. The proportion of full-time students is rising somewhat faster, from about one-third of total enrollment in the early 1960s to 43 percent in the IACP's 1968 survey. From campus to campus, however, enrollments range from exclusively full-time to exclusively part-time.

The proportional increase in full-time students has great potential significance for the future of law enforcement programs, but for the present, its meaning is not entirely clear. To date, the majority of nonpolice graduates of both two-year and four-year programs have apparently not entered the police service: through 1967, two-year programs had produced a total of 4,650 graduates who were not previously employed in law enforcement, and less than half of these are known to have entered the field. The total number of baccalaureate graduates stood at 4,457, less than a third of whom have since entered law enforcement.[41] Although some of the rest may eventually join police departments after military service or further formal education, most seek careers in federal or state investigative agencies, which offer higher status

40. Thompson S. Crockett, "Two Year Degree Programs in Law Enforcement" (processed; St. Petersburg Junior College, 1965).

41. Thompson S. Crockett, *Law Enforcement Education: A Survey of Colleges and Universities Offering Degree Programs in the Field of Law Enforcement* (International Association of Chiefs of Police, 1968).

and salaries, or in related occupations in the field of criminal justice.

For the police service, these statistics are cause for concern. They suggest that rising enrollments and expanding degree programs may have less of an impact on police manpower than might be expected. Whereas inservice enrollments measure the development of present personnel, preservice enrollments must be translated into entry before they have any effect on the quantity or quality of personnel. Collegiate programs will not realize their vast potential for upgrading police manpower until a larger proportion of these graduates enter the profession. And the proportion is unlikely to increase substantially until law enforcement agencies throughout the nation begin to make the changes necessary to attract better-qualified men.

Police programs in four-year institutions have status problems which do not exist in the community colleges, where occupational programs have a central role in the institutional mission. On the four-year campus, the greater the occupational emphasis of an undergraduate program, the less likely it is to be accepted by the other academic disciplines. Like schools of education in earlier decades, departments of law enforcement are not generally held in high esteem. Able students motivated toward a career in public service are apt to feel more comfortable in the other social sciences. No other college department so consistently reaches into the pool of practitioners for its faculty, and this tends to separate teachers of law enforcement from their colleagues. Their isolation is reinforced by a general failure to undertake research, the essential component in maintaining academic credentials for any discipline. Accordingly, baccalaureate law enforcement programs suffer from "academic dryness or lack of nourishment. Course offerings change little and chew over and over the standard fare with comparatively infrequent introduction of the new." [42]

The thinness of academic research on law enforcement prob-

42. William P. Brown, "The Police and the Academic World," *Police Chief,* Vol. 32 (May 1965), p. 9.

lems is not solely attributable to the police professors. Small departments, heavy teaching loads, and scarcity of funds have effectively denied them the opportunity to pursue research. Until recently, other disciplines such as sociology, political science, public administration, psychology, and law, which have a direct concern with the role of the police in society, have given it little research attention. The *Public Administration Review* carried only two articles concerned with the police from 1939 to 1967, while the *American Political Science Review* has had no articles dealing with the police in democratic societies for twenty years.[43] Between 1940 and 1965 only six articles on the police appeared in the *American Sociological Review* and the *American Journal of Sociology.*[44]

The police community must share equal blame for its neglect of research, however. In an era of rapid changes in their role and responsibilities and increasing public concern for the effectiveness of law enforcement, local police agencies have slighted their own research capacity and have hardly begun to explore the possibilities for cooperative research with the academic world:

> They have been concerned almost exclusively with using the colleges to transmit the rather meager supply of information which has been gathered by the police over the years. They have almost entirely neglected the areas of knowledge production and mastery and these constitute the absolute essences of any deeply rooted academic discipline.[45]

SOME HOPEFUL SIGNS

The problems of collegiate law enforcement programs must be considered in context. Many of the deficiencies are temporary manifestations of rapid and vigorous growth. A diversity of pro-

43. Noted by Jameson W. Doig in "Police Problems, Proposals, and Strategies for Change," *Public Administration Review*, September–October 1968, p. 402.
44. Cited as an illustration of "tragic and shameful neglect" by Robert Sheehan in "Police Education and Training," paper presented at the Tufts Assembly on Massachusetts Government sponsored by the Lincoln Filene Center for Citizenship and Public Affairs, Tufts University, 1968 (processed).
45. Brown, "The Police and the Academic World," p. 9. The fragmentation which characterizes the police system is of course another important deterrent to the development of a research capacity.

grams may be expected in such a newly developed field, and to a certain extent diversity should be encouraged.

It is unrealistic and perhaps undesirable to expect a single pattern of police education to emerge in the near future. The needs of the service are diverse: as the President's Commission on Law Enforcement suggested, police departments must learn to attract persons with a variety of specialized backgrounds, such as fiscal experts, engineers, scientists, planners and researchers, lawyers, and public administrators. All local agencies need to attract recruits with the qualities of intellect and character that will cnable them to understand and competently perform the law enforcement task, but such men must be drawn from the total spectrum of society rather than from any narrow segment of it. These requirements imply a continuing need for several varieties and levels of educational programs for preservice students. The educational needs of inservice police will also continue to vary, according to the makeup of individual departments and the particular needs of each community. As local agencies improve their training programs, there will be less reason for academic programs to perform this function.

Where local departments are poorly staffed and trained, the community college may have to supply the needed training, entirely consistently with its broad mission. Vocationally oriented police programs may meet a real need and, where appropriate, they may actually stimulate enrollment in academic programs. One authority has suggested that the occupational emphasis of many current programs is transitional, and that they are likely to become more academically oriented as the value of higher education for police becomes better understood.[46] The continued growth of baccalaureate programs is likely to contribute to the greater emphasis on general education in two-year degree programs, as junior colleges come under increasing pressure to provide credit offerings which are fully transferable toward a higher de-

46. James D. Stinchcomb, "The Community College and Its Impact," *Police Chief*, Vol. 33 (August 1966).

gree. In addition, growing national concern for the inadequacies of police training should lead to better training programs within local agencies and thereby reduce confusion over the role of the campus programs.

Another hopeful sign is the relatively recent but increasing interest of the academic community in the problems of criminal justice. August Vollmer's conclusion that "legislators should require State universities and colleges to establish Criminology Schools" has gone unheeded for two decades, and the record shows that "colleges and universities have long ignored the problems and educational needs of law enforcement." [47] But the currents of change are beginning to shape a new alliance between the police and the campus. This is partly due to the infusion of federal funds, but it is also due to a growing awareness that colleges and universities have a responsibility to help society deal with the massive problems of urban blight, poverty, and crime. Educational leadership is increasingly recognizing a broader public service mission. As one university president has observed, ". . . It is no longer enough to educate the men who will, in turn, serve society; the American university itself has now become an instrument for direct social action." [48]

Philanthropic foundations are also coming to support the developing alliance between the police and the academic community. A Ford Foundation grant in 1964 enabled the International Association of Chiefs of Police to provide assistance in curriculum planning and development of degree programs at colleges and universities throughout the country and led to the formation of IACP's Education and Training Section "to promote a more intimate and meaningful relationship between the police executive

---

47. Vollmer, *The Criminal* (Foundation Press, 1949), p. 447; U.S. President's Commission on Law Enforcement, *Task Force Report: The Police*, p. 128.
48. Homer D. Babbidge, Jr., quoted by John J. Corson in "Public Service and Higher Education: Compatibility or Conflict?" in *Whose Goals for American Education*, ed. Charles G. Dobbins and Calvin B. T. Lee (American Council on Education, 1968), p. 89. See also Edward D. Rhe's chapter on "Education in the Nation's Service" in the same volume.

and the police educator." Under a grant from the Kellogg Foundation, the American Association of Junior Colleges has taken the
first step toward the development of common criteria for two-year
programs. A special committee of educators and law enforcement
authorities helped draw up the AAJC's published guidelines,
which outlined desirable curriculum patterns and discussed the
needs and problems involved in organizing and staffing effective
programs.

Further impetus toward recognized standards was provided by
the IACP's 1968 endorsement of the AAJC guidelines and its
presentation of specific criteria for quality programs at the two-
year level:

> At least 90% of the program must transfer to a senior institution
> toward a baccalaureate degree in the criminal justice field.
>
> No more than one-third of the program should be made up of pro-
> fessional courses.
>
> The balance of the program should be heavily oriented toward the
> behavioral sciences and communications.
>
> Skill courses should not be included in the professional content,
> but may be used to meet physical education requirements.
>
> No credit should be allowed for police training or experience.
>
> All instructors of professional content courses should hold at least
> a baccalaurcate degree in addition to other qualifications.[49]

No matter how specific such guidelines may be, however, they
are only advisory. No institution is under obligation to implement
them or to endorse the general principles on which they were
formulated. No professional organization is empowered to identify institutions which maintain high standards or to penalize
those which do not. Most occupations which aspire to professional
status create mechanisms for the establishment and enforcement
of educational standards. Health technology programs, for example, are subject to a system of voluntary, extralegal accreditation conducted cooperatively by professional and educational

49. Crockett, *Law Enforcement Education*, p. 1.12.

groups. The institutions and organizations jointly agree on standards for degree programs, including general principles of organization and administration, essential services and facilities, faculty qualifications, curriculum content, and course sequence. These self-policing bodies accredit new health technology programs and work to strengthen existing programs through periodic review.[50] The system is reinforced by legal regulation of health workers by means of state statutes and regulatory boards and by professional bodies which certify the competency of entering personnel and approve health facilities.

Institutions of higher education must meet the general accreditation requirements of state departments of education, and they have long maintained their own system of voluntary regional accreditation to insure that all degree-granting institutions meet certain minimum requirements. But law enforcement programs are still too new to have received much attention in the accrediting process. Many programs would have difficulty surviving close scrutiny by the regional commissions, which hold as a minimum standard that "an institution offering specialized post–secondary school education may qualify for membership as an institution of higher education if such a specialty rests upon a base of liberal education required of all or most students." [51] Even if accrediting teams were to include educators qualified to evaluate law enforcement programs, they would be relatively powerless to bring about improvements except on a school-by-school basis until the police and the academic community adopt the kind of cooperative standards which have just been described for the health professions.

At present, there are serious obstacles to achievement of the recommendations for police education made by the President's

50. Requirements for degree programs in the health technology fields are discussed in detail in *A Guide for Health Technology Program Planning* (National Health Council and American Association of Junior Colleges, 1967).

51. *Procedures of Regional Associations in Accrediting Institutions of Higher Education* (National Commission on Accrediting, 1966), p. 4.

Commission on Law Enforcement. Police officials have cause to doubt the value received when they encourage their men to seek higher education or when they recruit graduates of degree programs. Educators have grounds for similar doubts about the place of law enforcement among other academic disciplines. Clarification of the objectives of degree programs and enunciation of standards are necessary to give both parties a better understanding of their roles and responsibilities and of the proper distinction between education and training. Law enforcement agencies must come to recognize that they have sole responsibility for teaching their personnel the basic skills and techniques of police work, and that this responsibility must not be delegated to the colleges. For their part, academic institutions must meet more satisfactorily their responsibility to the police student, which is no different from their responsibility to any student, namely, to foster his intellectual development and to give him a sound background for understanding modern society and his role in it.[52]

Progress toward higher training standards within the police service should alleviate some of the problems of police education. But even the most effective training programs would not reduce the need for college-level education. Increasingly higher educational levels will probably be needed for upward mobility in the police service of the future. In any case, it would be unrealistic to expect an absolute division between training and education, because the best of each will always contain elements of the other. Alfred North Whitehead's dictum applies as much to law enforcement as to any other field: "There can be no adequate technical training which is not liberal, and no liberal education which is not technical: that is, no education which does not impart both technique and intellectual vision."[53] Recalling Whitehead's

---

52. For a discussion of the respective roles of training and education, see Vern L. Folley, "The Sphere of Police Education," *Law and Order*, Vol. 15 (February 1967).

53. *The Aims of Education* (Mentor Books, 1953), p. 58.

words, one police educator observed that there are not one but two equally valid answers to the question, "How do you educate policemen?"—first, teach them "like anyone else"; and second, "teach them the practices, techniques, needs, and milieu of police work." [54] The college must give them the former kind of education and in the process a partial orientation to the latter.

54. Leonard E. Reisman, "How Do You Educate a Policeman?" *AAUW Journal* (May 1967), p. 188.

CHAPTER FIVE

Police Training

WHEN A COMMUNITY experiences a crisis in law enforcement, the need for trained policemen is suddenly apparent to everyone. Heightened racial tensions bring instant demands for training in riot control measures and community relations; sharp local increases in narcotics traffic, burglary, or other crimes bring pressures to improve police skills in these areas. Barring such crises, however, citizens show little concern for police training. Police budgets ordinarily contain little money for formal training, and from one year to the next, policemen receive little instruction aimed at increasing their competence.

On a majority of smaller police forces, in fact, the training of a recruit differs little from that described by a metropolitan chief four decades ago to the Wickersham Commission:

> I say to him that now he is a policeman, and I hope he will be a credit to the force. I tell him he doesn't need anybody to tell him how to enforce the law, that all he needs to do is to go out on the street and keep his eyes open. I say: "You know the Ten Commandments, don't you? Well, if you know the Ten Commandments, and you go out on your beat, and you see somebody violating one of those Ten Commandments, you can be pretty sure he is violating some law."

The commission found this procedure to be "rather characteristic" in most cities of the early 1930s, while in towns (below 10,000 population) "there is absolutely nothing done which by any stretch of the imagination could be considered as police training." [1]

Today, about one-quarter of all cities and half of the small towns still do nothing to train new recruits, unless it is to refer them to the Ten Commandments. Only a small minority of agencies providing training do so upon entry; the vast majority send new men out on the street immediately and train them—if at all—"as soon as possible" within their first year.

Once an officer has passed the recruit stage, he is unlikely to receive further training to maintain or improve his general competence or to qualify him for specialized assignment or promotion. Few departments conduct systematic inservice training for all personnel, and fewer still provide formal management training for those entrusted with administrative and supervisory responsibilities.

Apparently, an untrained police force is a scandal which most local governments are willing to tolerate, and most citizens are willing to ignore. Why this is so is far from obvious. "Where untrained persons are permitted to function as policemen, no person's life or liberty is safe," August Vollmer warned. [2] For more than three decades the need for training has been dramatized on a national scale by the Federal Bureau of Investigation and its director, J. Edgar Hoover, who has repeatedly stressed that

> the efficiency of law enforcement today is commensurate with the degree of training of its officers. Only through modern police training can we keep abreast of the times in the unceasing fight against lawlessness. . . . Police work by untrained men . . . is as obsolete as the practice of medicine by sorcery. [3]

It would seem logical for local governments to insist on a minimal level of training simply to assure that the police are able to

1. National Commission on Law Observance and Enforcement [Wickersham Commission], *Report on Police* (Government Printing Office, 1931), No. 14, pp. 66, 70.
2. Vollmer, *The Police and Modern Society* (University of California Press, 1936), p. 231.
3. Quoted by Albert Deutsch in "Is Your Police Force Obsolete?" *Colliers,* Oct. 1, 1954.

operate mechanically for their own safety and that of the public. More important than the issue of safety, however, is the fundamental question of competent and efficient job performance. "No person, regardless of his individual qualifications, is prepared to perform police work on native ability alone," the President's Commission Task Force on Police emphasized.[4] Even if the recruit possesses the highest qualities of intelligence, judgment, and emotional fitness, he still needs extensive training before he can understand the police job and develop the skills needed to perform it.

Moreover, the nature of the job will require that he receive periodic training throughout his career. Training needs grow, and new needs appear, in response to changes in technology and in society itself. Scientific advances may call for new investigative procedures, revised operating procedures, and familiarity with more sophisticated equipment. Changing social aspirations, values, and behavioral patterns may create tensions between races, generations, and interest groups which the policeman must be aware of and understand if he is to deal with potentially explosive situations fairly and effectively. From time to time legislatures and the courts may impose new standards and limitations on the performance of his functions. Criminals may be apprehended or escape, lives may be saved or lost, cities may be pacified or burned, and precedents affecting the work of policemen everywhere may be affected by the way an individual officer is trained to perform his duties.

It is not simply a question of providing training in those agencies which do not have it. The training conducted in most police departments fails to meet minimum standards of adequacy even in terms of hours of instruction. Nor is length of training a sufficient measure of adequacy. Training quality has received relatively little analysis, but available data suggest that the content and

4. U.S. President's Commission on Law Enforcement and Administration of Justice, *Task Force Report: The Police* (Government Printing Office, 1967), p. 137.

methods of instruction are grossly deficient in most agencies. Serious deficiencies have been observed in the programs provided in the best departments, in the most respected state and regional academies, and in the FBI's prestigious National Academy. All told, the training needs of local agencies are such that "another decade of total effort will be needed to raise police preparation to a uniform level of minimum adequacy," a study by the International Association of Chiefs of Police estimates.[5]

This chapter will examine the gap between the amount and quality of training currently available and that needed to reach the minimum standards recommended by the President's Commission on Law Enforcement. The extent of the gap will suggest some conclusions about the role of training in a national strategy to improve the effectiveness of law enforcement.

Recruit Training

The objective of recruit training is to equip all entering personnel with the essential skills and understanding required for competent performance on the job. To accomplish this, the President's Commission on Law Enforcement declared, recruit training "in all departments, large and small, should consist of an absolute minimum of 400 hours of classroom work spread over a 4- to 6-month period so that it can be combined with a carefully selected and supervised field training." The program should not only provide sufficient training in mechanical skills, it should also stress "subjects that prepare recruits to exercise discretion properly, and to understand the community, the role of the police, and what the criminal justice system can and cannot do."[6] But while specialists may accept these objectives, little agreement

5. George W. O'Connor, "Police Training," Report for the President's Commission on Law Enforcement and the Administration of Justice (processed; IACP, 1966), p. 1.

6. U.S. President's Commission on Law Enforcement and Administration of Justice, *The Challenge of Crime in a Free Society* (Government Printing Office, 1967), p. 112.

exists among police agencies throughout the country on what skills and understanding are essential for the recruit, and how they can best be inculcated. Even if a consensus were achieved on the length and content of training, the demanding nature of the law enforcement task itself would continue to challenge the effectiveness of even the most comprehensive training programs.

LENGTH OF TRAINING

Although some form of recruit training is now standard practice in larger cities, 18 percent of all municipal departments still provide no training at all. A 1967 survey (using Bureau of the Census categories) of cities of over 10,000 population found that 7 percent of departments in central cities, 11 percent of those in suburbs, and 32 percent of those in independent cities do not offer recruit training. This lack is common to all regions: 35 percent of departments in the southern states, and over 10 percent of departments in the northeast, north central, and western states, do not provide training.[7] The percentages are significantly higher when municipalities of under 10,000 population are included: a more extensive survey in 1965 found no recruit training in 31 percent of police agencies in New England, 21 percent of those in the middle Atlantic states, 42 percent in the east north central region, 36 percent in the west north central states, 42 percent in the south Atlantic states, 55 percent in the east south central states, 51 percent in the west south central states, 39 percent in the mountain states, and 24 percent in the Pacific states.[8] Another study of sheriff's departments in eleven southern states has reported that 56 percent offer no basic training for deputies from any source, and less than 20 percent conduct their own training programs.[9]

7. Robert J. Havlick, "Police Recruit Training," in *Municipal Yearbook, 1968* [International City Managers' Association, Chicago], p. 339.
8. George W. O'Connor, "Police Training," Tables 9 and 10.
9. Dana B. Brammer and James E. Hurley, "A Study of the Office of Sheriff in the United States, Southern Region, 1967" (processed; University of Mississippi, Bureau of Governmental Research, 1967), pp. 172–73.

Less than 15 percent of all agencies surveyed by IACP in 1965 provided immediate training for recruits; about half provided it "as soon as possible" within the first year. In almost 75 percent of the agencies providing training, it consisted of less than 200 hours. Most cities with less than 100,000 population offered less than 200 hours; a majority of larger cities provided more.[10] But only the largest offered 400 or more hours, and only a few of these met the criterion of the President's Commission on Law Enforcement that training be spread over a 4- to 6-month period.

The larger cities, of course, contain the bulk of the nation's police, and therefore a majority of all newly appointed officers actually undergo training at some time during their first year on the force. Nevertheless, recruits in most communities do not begin to receive the amount of training which the President's Commission judged to be the absolute minimum.

TRAINING CONTENT

No single training curriculum would be adequate for all communities. The content and conduct of instruction will necessarily vary according to local conditions and the strengths and weaknesses of the recruits, the instructional staff, and the facilities. At the same time, several broad areas can be identified as representing a core of knowledge and skills which should be conveyed to all new officers before they are entrusted with the lives and security of the citizenry. This core may be described as follows:

Administration of justice: foundations of criminal justice, state and federal constitutions, state criminal statutes, local codes and ordinances, court systems and procedures, laws of arrest, search, and

10. O'Connor, "Police Training," Table 1. Some improvement is indicated in the results of a more limited IACP training survey in 1968 (unpublished). For 439 departments responding, the average number of hours of recruit training was 293 hours for classroom work and field work combined. Averages ranged from 231 hours in cities of 10,000–25,000 to 486 hours in cities of over 250,000. But progress remains uneven. Regionally, average hours varied from 210 in the Northeast states to 361 in the Pacific states. Smaller cities in the West North Central region averaged only 150 hours; cities of 25,000–50,000 in the Northeast averaged 177 hours, and cities of 50,000–100,000 in the same region averaged only 196—compared with an average of 367 hours for cities of the same size in the Pacific states.

seizure, testimony in court, rules of evidence, the functions and duties of criminal justice agencies, juvenile court procedures, civil rights, civil law.

Patrol procedures: patrol techniques, preliminary investigations, report writing, communication procedures, responding to calls for service, handling criminal cases, noncriminal cases, and disaster cases.

Traffic enforcement: state and local traffic codes, traffic direction, officer-violator contacts, summons issuance procedures, traffic court procedures, accident investigation, drunk-driving cases.

Social science: basic psychology, abnormal psychology, human relations, crime and delinquency causation, geography, public relations.

Investigation: conduct of interviews, interrogation, case preparation, investigation of crimes against persons, investigation of crimes against property, organized crime and vice, crime scene procedures, collection of evidence, scientific crime detection, personal identification.

Emergency medical services: basic first aid, emergency childbirth, recognition and handling of the mentally disturbed.

Physical training and skills: proper use of firearms, defensive tactics, mechanics of arrest, crowd and riot control, prisoner transportation.

Agency standards and procedures: department rules and regulations, code of ethics, general and specific orders, jail procedures, records procedures, vehicle and equipment care and use, department organization, personnel procedures.

Most training programs give at least cursory attention to each of these subjects, but the number of hours devoted to each varies widely, and none can generally be said to receive adequate treatment. The President's Commission Task Force on Police judged that "the vocational training needs of recruits are inadequately met in most departments." [11] Other investigators have found that even the more extensive programs provide inadequate training in

11. U.S. President's Commission on Law Enforcement, *Task Force Report: The Police*, p. 138.

some of the basic elements of police work. The IACP, for example, made the following criticisms of the 456-hour recruit training program conducted by the District of Columbia:

> The curriculum is deficient in material on the conduct of preliminary investigations by patrol officers, and there are no course titles dealing with the collection and preservation of physical evidence. There is no course on patrol methods, including preventive patrol, inspectional service, and field interrogations. Little is presented on the handling of miscellaneous police cases and common misdemeanors, particularly the incidents most likely to be encountered by patrol officers—abandoned cars, assaults, casualty cases, drunkenness, family fights, juvenile disturbances, runaway juveniles, noise complaints, suspicious circumstances investigations, and prowler calls.[12]

A study of recruit training in another large metropolitan force found that only 1 hour out of 490 was devoted to the handling of domestic disturbances, although the teaching outline acknowledged that disturbance calls outnumbered any other type received by individual officers.[13] The National Advisory Commission on Civil Disorders found critical deficiencies in the riot control training given recruits in most large cities.[14] The IACP has reported "obvious weakness" in training for the handling of juveniles:

> ... The amount of time spent in recruit training on juvenile matters ranges from 0 to 5 percent of the recruit course, the median being between 1 and 2 percent. ... This is a rather unimpressive picture in the light of the increase in juvenile crime during the past several years. ... In view of the volume of cases, the inevitability of patrol contacts with juveniles, and the potential for preventive police work by all officers, existing programs are obviously inadequate.[15]

A scholar who has analyzed programs in several major departments and police academies concluded that training is generally not sufficiently grounded in the realities of day-to-day operations:

12. *Report of the President's Commission on Crime in the District of Columbia* (Government Printing Office, 1966), Appendix, p. 151.
13. Herman Goldstein, "Police Response to Urban Crisis," *Public Administration Review*, Vol. 28 (September–October 1968).
14. *Report of the National Advisory Commission on Civil Disorders* (Government Printing Office, 1968), p. 270.
15. Nelson A. Watson and Robert N. Walker, "Training Police for Work with Juveniles" (processed; IACP, 1965), p. 4.

... The training [the recruit] often receives in the academies today—if he receives any training at all—has largely to do with the penal code, with how to make out reports, and how to be an effective investigator of serious crimes—murders, arsons, burglaries—which occupy a very small fraction of the total police workload. . . .[16]

One reason why training so often fails to prepare officers for the realities of police work is that it seldom includes street experience. Fifty-eight percent of all departments in cities of over 10,000 population have no field training for recruits,[17] and most of the rest give it after formal classroom work is concluded. Only a handful of agencies integrate classroom study with the kind of formal, carefully supervised field training recommended by the President's Commission on Law Enforcement. The potential importance of such training, or the lack of it, has been emphasized by the IACP:

Recruits do better if they have some street experience during basic training, if for no other reason than to find out what they need to know. Material is much more readily absorbed when it can be related to past experience. . . . The influence of field training is even more profound than recruit school. The early working experience with another police officer will have a lasting influence on an officer's remaining service to the Department. If there is no normal field training program, or if the selection of field training officers is left to chance, the recruit will be simply exposed to a variety of experiences without gaining any significant understanding of them. If the older officer himself is incompetent, his incompetence will rub off on the younger man and mediocrity will be perpetuated. If the older man's attitude or philosophy is at variance with that of the profession, a disaffected, disloyal or disinterested recruit may be produced. If the older man's integrity is not absolute, and if the new recruit sees evidence of it, the new man can conceivably be a continuing problem to the Department as long as he is on the rolls.[18]

16. James Q. Wilson, testimony before the National Advisory Commission on Civil Disorders, Sept. 22, 1967 (p. 1762 of unpublished transcript).

17. Havlick, "Police Recruit Training," p. 349 (Table 14). An unpublished IACP training survey in 1968 found that field training for recruits varied from 2 hours to 480 hours and averaged 72 hours in departments which provide it.

18. *Report of the President's Commission on Crime in the District of Columbia,* Appendix, p. 153.

However thoroughly a program teaches vocational skills, it is seriously deficient if it concentrates on mechanical procedures and techniques to the exclusion of broader aspects of the police task. The President's Commission on Law Enforcement confirmed a generalization made fifteen years earlier about American police schools, that they teach the officer "everything except the essential requirements of his calling, which is how to secure and maintain the approval and respect of the public whom he encounters daily in the course of his duties." [19] The commission found that most departments still fail to prepare a recruit for this vital aspect of his job. Even in programs of 400 hours or longer, only a few hours are typically devoted to the subject of relationships with the community and examination of its problems, particularly those of race relations. As a former New York City police commissioner has testified,

> We cannot continue to be satisfied with a trade school approach to police training. The police officer must be instructed in human relations, civil rights, constitutional guarantees. In short, he has to be prepared to assume his role as a social scientist in the community.[20]

In all cities and towns, no matter what their size, location, or metropolitan status, the emphasis in training is overwhelmingly on such topics as law or traffic. These receive 8 hours of attention for every 2 devoted to police-community relationships, according to a recent survey, which notes: "This would seem to indicate a lack of responsiveness on the part of police training programs to the social convulsions occurring in today's cities. . . . Even in the central cities where most of the police and community friction has occurred one does not find a more intense training effort than in suburban and independent cities." [21]

Few training programs meet the test proposed by the President's Commission on Crime in the District of Columbia—that

19. Charles Reith, *The Blind Eye of History: A Study of the Origins of the Present Police Era* (Faber and Faber, Ltd., 1952), pp. 115–16.
20. Stephen P. Kennedy, a 1958 statement quoted in *U.S. Commission on Civil Rights Report*, Bk. 5: *Justice* (Government Printing Office, 1961), p. 86.
21. Havlick, "Police Recruit Training," p. 344.

they equip "the recruit to exercise his discretion wisely when confronted with actual enforcement problems." [22] Nor do most programs provide adequate material on the history of law enforcement and the role of the police in modern society. After reviewing training programs in a variety of agencies across the nation, the President's Commission Task Force on Police concluded: "... It remains doubtful whether even a majority of them provide recruits with an ample understanding of the police task." [23]

PROBLEMS OF RECRUIT TRAINING

Developing an adequate recruit program is a difficult assignment for any department, regardless of its capacities and its leadership's convictions about the importance of training. If the smallness of a department or the unavailability of qualified instructors does not create practical problems, the complex nature of the police task will itself inevitably raise questions of training strategy and theory which are difficult to resolve under the best of circumstances.

Size. The size of the community has an important effect on the amount of training provided for entering recruits. Virtually all larger cities conduct training of some duration, whereas less than one-quarter of cities with less than 50,000 population maintain their own programs. Smaller forces generally do not have the resources to sustain lengthy training and feel they cannot send working patrolmen away to neighboring cities or area academies without seriously depleting their strength. In some rural communities, there may not be enough crime to justify the additional expense of training in the eyes of local officials.

Although rural and suburban police customarily receive less training than their big-city counterparts, the policemen on the smaller force may actually have greater training needs. Metropolitan agencies have detectives to take over major investigations, and

22. *Report of the President's Commission on Crime in the District of Columbia*, p. 177.
23. U.S. President's Commission on Law Enforcement, *Task Force Report: The Police*, p. 138.

juvenile officers, laboratory technicians, photographers, and other specialists are available as needed. By comparison, small-town agencies usually recruit from a smaller manpower pool, maintain less rigid entrance standards, and do not have a staff of specialists. Their patrolmen thus have less preparation to undertake a greater range of responsibilities. The need for well-trained police may seem less urgent in smaller jurisdictions, but it is always potentially present.

The size of a community need not limit the adequacy of the training it provides its police. Departments which are too small to conduct their own training may send new recruits to metropolitan, state, or regional police academies or make arrangements with area community colleges to provide training before they are assigned to patrol duty.

Quality of Instruction. The President's Commission on Law Enforcement found instruction in most departments to be inadequate. It suggested that all regular instructors be required to complete a teacher training course of at least 80 hours, as demanded by the FBI of its agents assigned to teach. Police instructors rarely receive any such training; they are drawn from the regular ranks with little regard for previous teaching experience or ability. Almost two-thirds of all police instructors have not had any post– high school education.[24] Their lack of pedagogical training is evident in their performance. Instruction often consists of little more than a series of unrelated talks on various aspects of police work.

There is a common belief within the service that "it takes a policeman to teach a policeman," with the result that the use of civilian specialists is limited. When guest speakers are invited, their presentation is seldom integrated with the rest of the course material. As a consequence

> ... student attention and discipline are sometimes deficient during guest lectures. In some training schools, students begin to believe

24. Unpublished IACP training survey of 1968.

that the material handed out by outsiders is considered by the training staff to be either inconsequential or controversial.[25]

The President's Commission recommended that professional educators and civilian experts be used to teach specialized courses such as law and psychology and that their material be carefully integrated into the training curriculum.

The commission found that police instructors typically use antiquated training methods. Recent data suggest that a variety of educational techniques such as television, field observation, and discussion of assigned readings are coming into general use in most cities, but lectures remain the dominant method of instruction.[26]

Training Strategy. The training program also serves as a battleground in the struggle for reform of the police service. The instructor's pedagogical skills are not the only question at issue; his outlook may be a significant factor in molding the attitudes and understanding of recruits. In assigning training officers, the police establishment is more likely to select defenders of the system than critics of it. Some scholars view this as a major weakness of police schools:

The most significant qualification for a police instructor . . . is his stand on the great social issues of the day that relate to police: poverty, housing, race, integration, and police-community relations. Those defenders of past practices who insist that nothing is wrong with the present system should never be given an opportunity to teach policemen. There is much wrong with the present system, and some horrendous things have gone on in the past. Someone who fails to understand the implications of this or who refuses to admit, even to himself, that there is plenty of room for progress cannot possibly teach men to better the system and make it a more effective and acceptable instrument of progressive social change.

The police instructor who really meets his responsibilities and obligations must be a man who . . . will often be in direct conflict with the police practitioner. He must constantly be prepared for

25. *Report of the President's Commission on Crime in the District of Columbia,* Appendix, p. 150.
26. Havlick, "Police Recruit Training," p. 345.

challenge from a field which is resisting change so strenuously and is threatened so severely that it becomes outraged by criticism and stifles all dissent. For a police training program to be very effective in an atmosphere so hostile to change presents some real difficulties. . . .[27]

Perhaps the greatest difficulty is the disparity between the ethics, ideals, and theory taught in the academy and the actualities of everyday practice, which has been noted in numerous studies. Instructors who attempt to instill higher standards of professionalism are undermined by cynical veterans on the force who advise the recruit that "to become a real policeman, he will have to forget everything he is learning at the Academy." [28]

While conflict between theory and practice is present to some extent in any kind of professional training, it is accentuated in the case of the police. In fact, some instructors actually attempt to widen the gap between theory and practice because of their awareness of the need to upgrade police performance. Thus, at New York City's Police Academy, where all recruits receive four months of formal training for patrol duty in the precincts, discussion of many informal practices observable within the department is avoided by the faculty in order that they not appear to endorse evasion of the rules. Further, the work experience built into the program tends to emphasize clerical or janitorial duties rather than actual street experience, since academy personnel are reluctant to let recruits patrol with experienced officers for fear that they might be exposed to officially improper performance.[29]

27. Robert Sheehan, "Police Education and Training," paper presented at the Tufts Assembly on Massachusetts Government sponsored by the Lincoln Filene Center for Citizenship and Public Affairs, Tufts University, 1968 (processed).

28. Arthur Neiderhoffer, *Behind the Shield: The Police in Urban Society* (Doubleday, 1967), p. 44. The debunking process which recruits are subjected to following completion of training school and the stresses they undergo in modifying their book learning to actual enforcement practices are treated in *An Examination of Role Theory: The Case of the State Police*, by Jack J. Preiss and Howard J. Ehrlich (University of Nebraska Press, 1966), pp. 20–23.

29. John H. McNamara, "Uncertainties in Police Work: The Relevance of Police Recruits' Backgrounds and Training," in *The Police: Six Sociological Essays*, ed. David J. Bordua (John Wiley & Sons, 1967), p. 217.

Another problem of training strategy is raised by the recommendation of the President's Commission on Law Enforcement that recruits receive more preparation for exercising discretion:

> The organization of police departments and the training of policemen are focused almost entirely on the apprehension and prosecution of criminals. What a policeman does, or should do, instead of making an arrest or in order to avoid making an arrest, or in a situation in which he may not make an arrest, is rarely discussed. The peacekeeping and service activities, which consume the majority of police time, receive too little consideration.[30]

Such training may pose a serious threat to the traditional police organization: personnel trained to be self-directed and autonomous are unlikely to be content with the old ways. They will be more inclined to search for better ways of performing their task, siding with the reformers rather than the entrenched establishment. Few departments consciously select this training strategy. Instead, they opt for the more traditional emphasis of going by the book, aiming at the development of personnel who are readily subject to organizational control.

The alternatives of reform or tradition need not be mutually exclusive. One scholar has suggested that training strategy should occupy a middle ground: instead of viewing ideal police work as irreconcilable with actual practice, training personnel should

> make every effort to introduce what they consider ideal practice into the training in such a way that it does not call for a major scrapping of what the men in the field units consider to be "tried and true." In this way, the ideal practices would be less likely to call forth a defensive reaction from personnel who see their own position or their advantages as threatened by innovations. The net effect of such a strategy should be less subversion of academy training by experienced men in the field.[31]

Complexities of the Police Job. Many training deficiencies reflect the difficulties inherent in any effort to prepare recruits for their job. It is no simple matter to develop the capacity and moti-

30. U.S. President's Commission on Law Enforcement, *The Challenge of Crime in a Free Society*, p. 92.
31. McNamara, "Uncertainties in Police Work," pp. 251–52.

vation for competent performance throughout the full range of situations which policemen are likely to face. After studying the program offered by the New York City Police Academy—one of the most comprehensive in the nation—one scholar concluded that "in view of the demands placed on the individual officer it would seem unlikely that four months of formal training is sufficient" to develop the characteristics and skills needed for effective performance on foot patrol.[32] His examination of the academy's effect on the attitudes of several hundred policemen illustrates the problems which are built into even the most highly regarded training programs.

"The law" which police are sworn to enforce presents a major challenge. If an officer is to make decisions with any confidence in the correctness of his actions, he must have a sound grasp of procedural and substantive law. Accordingly, he is expected to memorize a vast body of federal, state, and local laws and judicial decisions. This emphasis on rote learning of the letter of the law encourages him to believe that the law is fixed and immutable, which may predispose him to seek extralegal methods of performing his job. It also tends to deny the large role of discretion in police work, leaving him unprepared to exercise his judgment.

Attempts to build esprit de corps among recruits tend to heighten their perception of the discrepancy between the policeman's status and his vital role in the community. This generates cynicism toward the police service and bitterness toward the public, reinforcing the tendency of police to function in secrecy. It also tends to weaken confidence in the values taught in the police academy. Thus, even the most carefully designed training program may not succeed in immunizing recruits against some of the attitudes that foster poor performance.

Such problems cannot be fully resolved without fundamental reforms of the police system. But they cannot even begin to be

32. *Ibid.*, p. 191. In 1969 the Chicago Police Department began to provide seven months of training for recruits, the longest and most comprehensive program in the nation, involving more than 1,000 classroom hours of instruction, including college-level courses in such subjects as sociology and psychology.

faced in most agencies until police and public officials insist that all recruits achieve minimum standards of competence before they are entrusted with the task of law enforcement.

Inservice Training

As in any skilled occupation, training must be a continuing process to maintain effective performance in law enforcement. Changes in the laws, in technology, and in the needs of the community make periodic retraining of all personnel essential. Old skills need sharpening with new knowledge and new techniques; specialized knowledge and skills must be taught for certain assignments or for promotion to higher responsibilities. The President's Commission on Law Enforcement recommended that "every general enforcement officer should have at least one week of intensive training a year," and specialized training should be made a prerequisite for advancement.[33]

Judged by the commission's standards, most police agencies are grossly deficient. Few departments anywhere provide systematic training for all personnel at all levels and in all areas of specialization. Except in the largest agencies, inservice training is "virtually negligible," the IACP reported to the commission.[34]

Of 54 police agencies in the Detroit metropolitan area, for example, the IACP found that less than one-third offered any training beyond recruit school and that this was usually limited to the brief period at roll call before going on duty. Another study has shown that only 21.6 percent of sheriff's departments in eleven southern states provided inservice training for their deputies.[35]

33. U.S. President's Commission on Law Enforcement, *The Challenge of Crime in a Free Society*, p. 113.

34. O'Connor, "Police Training," p. 21. Illustrating this point, a recent IACP Survey of 1220 police agencies found that 80 percent have issued chemical spray weapons, but only a third of them have provided instructions to govern their use. *New York Times*, Feb. 22, 1970.

35. Of departments without programs, 54 percent said their men received no inservice training from any outside source. Brammer and Hurley, "A Study of the Office of Sheriff in the United States Southern Region, 1967," pp. 174–75.

Most departments of any size provide some training. Hundreds of agencies make use of the skilled instruction offered by visiting FBI instructors, invite outside specialists to give occasional lectures, conduct periodic courses in specialized subjects, and send selected individuals to programs at state or regional police schools or universities. But only a minority of agency personnel are involved in these activities: although 81 percent of departments in one survey reported some kind of specialized training, 51 percent said that less than one-quarter of their entire force was involved, and only 13 percent reported involvement of over three-quarters of their men.[36]

Many of the difficulties involved in recruit training are also present in inservice training. There is the fundamental problem of designing programs to assure competence in the whole range of police skills. There is the problem of providing qualified instruction. There is the problem of resources—the smaller the community, the more limited the training is likely to be, despite the fact that its citizens deserve no less competent law enforcement. Most cities of less than 50,000 population do not maintain a training division or a full-time training officer, which means that in order to provide training they must share the programs offered by larger departments, convince the city fathers to underwrite the expenses of travel and attendance at police schools, or make do with a haphazard scheduling of visiting lecturers as they are available.

Discontinuity between classroom theory and actual practice is not a problem with inservice training. The emphasis in much specialized instruction is on sharpening mechanical skills, and in the case of promotional or management training, it is a question of broadening the understanding of men who are already experienced and knowledgeable. Yet the disparities in content and quality of programs are just as marked as in the case of recruit training, revealing a similar lack of consensus within the police

36. Raymond L. Bancroft, "Municipal Law Enforcement 1966," *Nation's Cities*, Vol. 4 (February 1966), p. 21.

service on what constitutes effective inservice training and even whether it is desirable. In fact, the deficiencies of inservice training may be more serious than those of recruit training because they are not as well recognized.

PROBLEMS OF QUALITY AND CONTENT

Comparative data on inservice training programs do not exist, but informed observers have consistently noted the poor quality of much of the training that is provided. Departmental programs have been characterized as "distinctly inferior" in all but a few instances.[37] Private and public commissions examining the status of law enforcement in cities or states inevitably find that existing programs fail to meet training needs.[38] The President's Commission on Law Enforcement observed a significant lack of balance in most training programs, particularly in the slighting of peacekeeping functions.

In every specific phase of training examined by competent authorities, serious weaknesses have been identified. Although most city departments now conduct some form of riot or crowd control training, the National Advisory Commission on Civil Disorders judged most of it to be critically deficient in substance:

> The Commission survey on the capabilities and preparedness of selected police departments showed that the most critical deficiency of all is inadequate training. Practically no riot control training is provided for supervisory police officers. Recruits receive an average of 18 hours in departments offering anywhere from 62 hours to only 2. Moreover, although riot control tactics require the work of highly disciplined and coordinated teams, almost all departments train policemen as individuals.
>
> Eleven of the 30 police departments surveyed reported no special or additional riot control training beyond the recruit level. Of the

37. Bruce Smith, *Police Systems in the United States* (2d rev. ed.; Harper & Row, 1960), p. 132.
38. See, for example, "The Police in Massachusetts," Report by the Governor's Committee on Law Enforcement and Administration of Justice, Dec. 21, 1967 (processed).

19 departments reporting some post-recruit training, five limit training to the use of firearms and chemicals. In many cases, the training program is built around traditional military formations that have little applicability to the kinds of disorders experienced in our cities.[39]

The same IACP study which revealed inadequate attention to the handling of juveniles in recruit training found that "time devoted to juvenile matters during inservice and supervisory training is even more disappointing." [40] Only 40 percent of 381 agencies surveyed in 1968 reported mandatory courses in human relations, and these varied from a low of 2 hours to a high of 80.[41] One former chief has expressed the view that "the greatest deficiency in police work today is that policemen themselves have only meager knowledge of what constitutes evidence and what they should do with evidence once it has been identified." [42] Although training in specialized techniques and procedures has become increasingly available in recent years, "our weakest link in law enforcement is the paucity of specially trained men and women," another commentator has declared.[43]

Some of the largest cities maintain extensive ongoing training activities. In Los Angeles, for example, all officers must return to school for 40–80 hours of general refresher training after their first year on the job, again between their third and fifth years, and again between their seventh and fourteenth years. The Chicago Police Department's Training Division conducts a continuing program of mandatory preservice and inservice training for patrolmen, specialists, and management personnel and also provides dozens of special courses, film strips, and other materials for use in all district stations and an extension program of correspondence

39. *Report of the National Advisory Commission on Civil Disorders,* p. 270.
40. Watson and Walker, "Training Police for Work with Juveniles," p. 4.
41. Unpublished IACP data.
42. Earle Roberts, former chief of Battle Creek, Mich., quoted by Robert Ostermann in *Crime in America* (National Observer Newsbook, 1966), p. 11.
43. Samuel Haig Jameson, "Controversial Areas in 20th Century Policing: Quest for Quality Training in Police Work," in *Interdisciplinary Problems in Criminology: Papers of the American Society of Criminology, 1964,* ed. Walter C. Reckless and Charles L. Newman (Ohio State University, 1965), p. 124.

courses. Most other major departments also conduct extensive training activities, although they are generally less comprehensive. IACP surveys illustrate the shortcomings of these activities. In Washington, D.C., for example, "the principal criticism is that the training has not reached sufficient numbers of people to be of consequence to the efficiency of the Department." The survey reported that the department's one-month advanced training course for veteran patrolmen largely duplicated the content of basic training and was only available to a relative few who had been recommended by their unit commanders. Other training activities conducted over a three-year period included a 48-hour course in prevention and control of juvenile delinquency, held periodically for selected officers; special courses for the Civil Disturbance Unit and the Canine Corps; a one-week supervisory course; a course in human relations for plainclothes officers and men with the rank of sergeant and above; and various lectures of one and two hours' duration. Roll-call training was theoretically provided in each unit. In some precincts it was extensive and imaginative; in most, however, "training consisted of the lieutenant or someone else reading Department orders." [44] Despite such inadequacies, the inservice training available in larger departments is obviously superior to that provided in most smaller agencies.

Formal promotional training is less generally available. Only 21 percent of 276 agencies surveyed in 1968 conducted mandatory training for all officers being promoted to higher responsibilities, as recommended by the President's Commission on Law Enforcement.[45] Little of this training was as substantial as the commission felt necessary; hours devoted to it ranged from 2 to 160.

44. *Report of the President's Commission on Crime in the District of Columbia,* Appendix, pp. 155–63.
45. Unpublished IACP data. A more extensive training survey in the same year obtained a slightly higher percentage: of 595 departments reporting, almost 30 percent provided some kind of preassignment training. But less than 14 percent provided training for promotion to lieutenant, and less than 10 percent for promotion to captain.

The commission also found that executive training was rarely provided, even in the largest departments. Yet training is equally necessary at the top ranks of a police department. Appointments to command echelons are made almost exclusively from the lower ranks, and basic training obviously does not prepare an individual to assume responsibilities for fiscal management, planning and research, general administration, or leadership of a major government agency.

The commission called for major expansion of the programs for training of upper and middle management personnel offered by the FBI National Academy, state and regional police schools, and various colleges and universities. A recent analysis of these programs concluded, however, that although the instruction provided is of high caliber, "a relatively small percentage of their total programs deal with the subject of professional police management." [46] The study questioned the relevance of National Academy programs to the needs of middle- and upper-management police officials invited to participate. It found that only 19 percent of the curriculum could be described as management training, the bulk of courses consisting of subjects more appropriate for recruit training, such as firearms and ballistics, photography, fingerprint identification, defensive tactics, criminal law, police records, and surveillance. Existing programs for police executives, moreover, reach only a small fraction of those in the top echelons.[47] In terms of the need for developing a more coherent philosophy of professional police management, a serious question may be raised about the value of programs which, in effect, provide top-quality basic training for only a relatively small proportion of management-level personnel.

46. Norman E. Pomrenke, "A Preliminary Survey of Police Management Training Needs and Facilities in Eight Southern States," Study for the Office of Law Enforcement Assistance, Department of Justice (processed, 1967), p. 70.

47. *Ibid.* The IACP's 1968 training survey (unpublished) found that 397 of 595 reporting departments participated in some form of national or regional training by sending one or more officers to the National Academy, the Southern Police Institute, the Northwestern Traffic Institute, or similar school. But attendance at

THE PROBLEM OF RECOGNIZING THE PROBLEM

The general lack of effective training at all levels of the police service may be more serious than the shortcomings of recruit training. But it is not as obvious, in part because progress in this area is more visible than in recruit training and because real progress has in fact been made. Inservice training did not exist until August Vollmer began the first program in his Berkeley department in 1908. The New York City Police Department established a training academy in 1909, and a few other municipalities organized their own schools in subsequent years, but it was not until the 1930s that the FBI focused national attention on the need for training in all agencies. In the same decade, a number of state police organizations opened their training programs to local police. The concept of daily roll-call training was pioneered in Los Angeles in 1948. Supervisory and administrative training was introduced in 1954. The first state laws setting training standards were enacted in 1959 in California and New York. College- and university-based training programs have only become widespread in the last decade. The IACP's strong leadership toward higher professional standards began in the early 1960s. Only within the last few years, under the impetus of the report of the President's Commission on Law Enforcement and the new availability of federal funds, has the law enforcement community begun to coordinate its efforts to improve training.[48]

Today, police training activities are under way at every level of government. State, regional, and national conferences, seminars, and workshops abound for law enforcement officials. Virtually all cities of over 50,000 population and three-quarters of cities of under 50,000 population now report some form of inservice train-

---

such programs varied widely according to the size and region of the department: only 45 percent of agencies in the Middle Atlantic states participated, and only 37 percent of agencies in cities of 10,000–25,000 population. The total number of men sent by the reporting agencies was 477 in 1967.

48. For a detailed history of the development of police training, see Allen Z. Gammage, *Police Training in the United States* (Charles C Thomas, 1963).

ing.[49] But such statistics are misleading, however encouraging they may be. As a measure of departments providing systematic training for all personnel, they are worthless. They include everything from an occasional filmstrip presented at roll call to specialized programs for a few individuals. The reported number of training hours varies from a low of 1 to a high of 280. The recent flurry of activity in a relatively few areas such as riot control and community relations does not begin to deal with the full scope of the training problem. The fact that some training is taking place may, as has been noted, detract attention from the relatively small percentage of personnel involved and the scarcity of programs which attempt to upgrade the performance of officers throughout the career structure.

That the extent of training deficiencies is not widely appreciated is in part the responsibility of the very agency which has unquestionably done more than any other to improve police training. The FBI's highly colored prose creates the distinct impression that the problem is under control:

> A hub of law enforcement experience and resources, the FBI is enthusiastically committed to the improvement of all levels of the profession. In this central role the FBI provides expert assistance to local, state and other Federal law enforcement agencies in a variety of specialized and vital areas in the harsh struggle with criminality. Apace with a galaxy of demands for improved qualifications, training and skills for police officers, the FBI has undertaken bold programs to better serve these needs. . . .
>
> . . . The FBI conducted an accelerated program of expert law enforcement instruction during the year. More than 1,000 highly trained and experienced FBI Special Agents from all sections of the United States provided training assistance for over 177,000 municipal, city, county and state law enforcement officers in a record 6,045 schools held throughout the Nation. . . .
>
> . . . The FBI National Academy has rightfully become known as the "West Point of Law Enforcement." Three thousand forty-four of

49. Data from an unpublished 1968 survey of 286 cities by the IACP

its graduates are still active in law enforcement, and over 27 percent of these occupy top executive positions in their agencies.

The National Academy is the summit of law enforcement training. Staffed with expert FBI instructors qualified to lecture in all areas of law enforcement obligations, the intensified 12-week curriculum is designed to prepare the student officer as an administrator or instructor in his own department. Among the advanced instruction given, recurring emphasis is placed on the human relations factor in law enforcement—a requisite ingredient of responsible and effective police performance. In the fiscal year, 200 officers, including a number from foreign countries, graduated from the FBI National Academy.[50]

Citizens, local officials, and legislators evidently find reassurance in these words. During debate on the omnibus crime bill, some congressmen repeatedly questioned the need for federal support of law enforcement training and actively opposed it on the grounds that

> this proposal fails to take into account the very extensive guidance and direction being given by the FBI in the whole area of law enforcement.... In many States it may be true, they may not have appropriate training, but all they have to do is ask the local office of the FBI and tell them what kind of information they want.... The FBI will send instructors there and give the schooling.[51]

The training offered by the FBI is not as impressive as it appears in the annual report, however. It should not be mistaken for comprehensive training. Most of the 6,045 "schools" mentioned in the report for fiscal year 1967 actually consisted of a few hours of lectures by visiting FBI agents, and the 177,000 officers reportedly "trained" were in fact the total number of patrolmen assembled to hear the lecturers. Although the agents' presentations are known to be of high quality, there is no way to judge the relevance of their material to the training needs of a particular

50. *FBI Annual Report Fiscal Year 1967* (Government Printing Office, 1967), p. 31.
51. H. Allen Smith (Republican of California) in *Congressional Record*, daily ed., Aug. 8, 1967, pp. H 10087–88.

audience. It seems unlikely that they could meet the needs of those departments which have no training programs of their own:

... There is as yet no assurance that the rather brief courses are of sufficient bulk to occupy a large place in the real training needs of small communities. Some of the most elementary of police techniques require much time for their proper description and demonstration.[52]

Nor can the FBI meet the training needs of police executives in its National Academy programs, even after completion of its new facilities at Quantico, Va., permits expansion of graduating classes from 200 to 1,200 annually. Neither can the other management training programs with a national enrollment of police executives such as the Southern Police Institute at the University of Louisville, Ky., which offers a 3-month course open on the basis of competitive examinations; the 9-month course in police management offered by the Traffic Institute of Northwestern University, Evanston, Ill.; or the shorter courses of 2 to 5 weeks offered by these institutions and by the Department of Police Administration of Indiana University, the Southwestern Law Enforcement Institute of the Southwestern Legal Foundation, Dallas, Tex., the Harvard University Business School, and the IACP. Of an estimated 14,590 command personnel in eight southern states, these institutions trained a total of only 320 officers in the three years from 1964 through 1966.

National and regional training facilities cannot alone fill the training need. They can only supplement the program of a particular state. Statistics reveal that the number of law enforcement personnel attending national and regional facilities is minimal in terms of total law enforcement personnel. It is not reasonable that any national or regional facility can train the vast numbers of law enforcement command personnel.[53]

Similarly, the few states which maintain programs for local police do not begin to meet actual training needs. Since 1959,

52. Smith, *Police Systems in the United States*, p. 286.
53. Pomrenke, "A Preliminary Survey of Police Management Training Needs and Facilities . . . ," p. 70.

Minnesota has offered a variety of courses in different regions of the state, including basic recruit training, specialized courses, and management training, but coverage of local officers is not yet complete and officials estimate that they have met only about half of the training needs.[54] Even the states with the best and most comprehensive programs are not yet able to provide training for all local officers.

When the scope of police needs is considered, it is apparent that the FBI could never supply enough speakers and expertise to provide adequate, systematic, continuing training for all departments. Even if such a solution were feasible, its desirability would be questionable. It would require a massive expansion and redirection of responsibilities for the federal law enforcement agency. More important, using the FBI as the primary agency for training would necessarily subject all local agencies to a degree of federal direction and would constitute a major step toward a national police force, a step that has long been vigorously opposed by leading law enforcement spokesmen, including J. Edgar Hoover.[55]

If some citizens and congressmen believe that the training problem can be left to the FBI, many police officials are even less concerned and apparently feel that the problem does not exist.

54. Willard B. Morris, "Minnesota's State Training Program for Local Law Enforcement," *State Government,* August 1966.

55. Some police officials are critical of the power the FBI already has to give or withhold its cooperation and favor from local agencies. Robert Conot, in *Rivers of Blood, Years of Darkness* (Bantam Books, 1967), relates how disagreement between J. Edgar Hoover and the late Chief William H. Parker resulted in a virtual banning of the Los Angeles Police Department from the National Academy—a fact which may have had some bearing on police performance during the Watts riots, since riot control training was at that time little known outside of the academy. Conot writes: "... Although most top men in the sheriff's department have been to the FBI Academy, no Los Angeles police officer has attended the Academy since 1950. Applicants from the LAPD are politely told that there is a waiting list of seven to ten years.... As the FBI Academy's policy is to permit attendance of police officers from all U.S. cities as well as friendly foreign countries, in Parker's own words, 'I guess we are an unfriendly foreign country'" (p. 236). Similarly, no officers of the Chicago Police Department were accepted by the FBI Academy during the entire tenure of reform-minded Commissioner O. W. Wilson. Chicago was "readmitted" in early 1968, six months after Wilson's retirement.

Fifty-two percent of sheriffs in eleven southern states in 1967 indicated satisfaction with the amount of training made available to their departments, although less than 20 percent of the departments surveyed provided basic training for their deputies and less than 22 percent offered inservice training.[56] A sample of over 1,000 police chiefs surveyed by the International City Managers' Association produced a similar result: only 50 percent agreed that there were inadequacies in their recruit training programs. Chiefs of central city agencies, which typically conduct more extensive training, admit deficiencies more readily than their colleagues from smaller departments. Most frequently mentioned inadequacies are shortness of the training period, imbalance of the curriculum, lack of a full-time training officer, lack of adequate instructors and facilities, and lack of controlled field training.[57]

Such findings illustrate the massive resistance to change which still characterizes much of the police service. Despite increasing emphasis on training in recent years, its importance is not yet recognized by a clear majority of the nation's chiefs. Several observers have noted the apathy and even opposition of many police administrators toward professional concepts of training, and their widely held belief that experience is the best teacher.[58] Rank-and-file policemen can be expected to have no greater respect for the training process than their superiors. Police unions, growing

56. Brammer and Hurley, "A Study of the Office of Sheriff in the United States, Southern Region, 1967," p. 175.

57. Havlick, "Police Recruit Training," p. 347.

58. For example, A. C. Germann, in his *Police Personnel Management* (Charles C Thomas, 1958), reports that "many police administrators consider initial training superfluous" (p. 126). More recently, however, there is evidence that minimal training standards have apparently gained general support. A survey for the President's Commission on Law Enforcement and Administration of Justice (O'Connor, "Police Training," p. 9 [Table 2]) reported that 1,881 police chiefs—94 percent of those who indicated that their states did not have mandatory training laws—agreed that such legislation was needed.

E. Wilson Purdy has commented on the value of experience: "Experience alone is not enough. Relied upon solely, it is the most expensive and inefficient teacher. The average police officer with twenty-five years of service may actually have one year of experience, twenty-five times" (Purdy, "Administrative Action To Implement Selection and Training for Police Professionalization," *Police Chief*, Vol. 32 [May 1965], p. 16).

in power and increasingly aggressive in their demands for better salaries, have never been known as ardent advocates of better training.[59]

Inadequate attention to training can rarely be blamed exclusively on the police establishment, however. The blame also lies with elected officials who fail to provide their citizens with adequate and competent law enforcement. Often chiefs are unable to obtain support for the kind of training they know is needed.

> To state one example which I think is fairly common, the chief is not permitted to train his personnel, either within the department or away, because the mayor will not permit it for budgetary or other reasons. Many chiefs have indicated to me that they have attempted to do more training, but have been unable to receive the authority....[60]

The failure of local government officials to insist on adequate police training may be partly explained (though not excused) by the public's generally low understanding of the complexities of the police task. Needs for education, housing, welfare, roads, and other public services are more widely recognized and receive an increasing share of the local budget. To meet rising demands for these services, the police have been sadly neglected. It is estimated that there has been no appreciable real increase in funds available to local police for the last six decades.[61] Even if citizens were genuinely anxious to "support their local police," most communities obviously do not have the means to do so. The public responsi-

---

59. For example, the Patrolmen's Benevolent Association of New York City, arguing its case for higher salaries in full-page newspaper advertisements (*New York Times*, Nov. 1, 1968), outlined the demanding requirements of the job without suggesting any need for training. Rather, the ad copy suggested, policemen are qualified for all their tasks by the simple procedure of taking an oath: "This man took an oath which makes him . . . a guidance counselor, a sociologist, a community relations expert . . . a child psychologist . . . an interpreter, an obstetrician...." Needless to say, none of these professions claim their members to be qualified by virtue of an oath.

60. Testimony of Patrick V. Murphy before the National Advisory Commission on Civil Disorders, Sept. 22, 1967 (p. 1793 of unpublished transcript).

61. David J. Bordua and Albert J. Reiss, Jr., "Law Enforcement," in *The Uses of Sociology*, ed. Paul F. Lazarsfeld, William H. Sewell, and Harold L. Wilensky (Basic Books, 1967), p. 287.

bilities of local and state governments have already exceeded the revenue resources at their disposal, and improvement in the level of police service will increasingly require federal assistance.

Setting Standards

Substantial federal assistance to local police agencies is not likely to be forthcoming until minimum standards of adequacy for selection and training are recognized and accepted generally by the police service. Many chiefs are not yet willing to accept minimum standards for training, and their attitudes may be ascribed as much to honest doubt as to stubborn opposition to change. Training officers have no great body of accepted and tested theory, validated knowledge, or professional educational experience on which to base their efforts. Little has been done within the police service or in the academic community to evaluate existing training and its effects on personnel and the quality of law enforcement. Developing a model curriculum for recruit training is relatively simple; authorities generally agree on the broad subjects which should be included, although they may differ on the length of time and amount of attention to be devoted to each. Inservice training, on the other hand, involves not so much a program as a process—a process of continuing training throughout an individual's career according to his needs and those of his department.

It is no wonder, then, that current training efforts vary so widely in subject matter, time allotted, organization, methods of instruction, and personnel. One early effort to establish criteria for a comprehensive training curriculum concluded that the task was impossible, given the present state of knowledge, and urged that "uncoordinated attempts at solving police training problems be organized, systematized, centralized, and given direction to achieve maximum results." [62]

62. Ralph Green, "Initial Curriculum Study" (processed; Law Enforcement Training Project, Police Training Commission, New Jersey Department of Education, 1967).

However limited the state of knowledge may be, some minimum level of standards must be adopted and imposed before any large-scale improvement in police training can be expected. The President's Commission on Law Enforcement, in one of its most important recommendations, declared: "Police standards commissions should be established in every State, and empowered to set mandatory requirements and to give financial aid to governmental units for the implementation of standards." [63] The commission urged that such bodies be given powers to set standards for selection, training, and certification of qualified police officers, to establish training programs where facilities were unavailable, to help local agencies finance their training, and to conduct research.

Since 1959, when the first training councils were established in California and New York, through 1968, 31 states had enacted standards legislation. Only 17 states, however, have made basic training mandatory for all officers, and in 2 of these, smaller agencies are specifically exempted.[64] Standards are voluntary in 14 states. Powers granted to state councils vary widely. Nineteen have authority to establish minimum standards for employment on probationary status; only 1 council sets standards for permanent appointments. Twenty-four councils are empowered to set minimum curriculum requirements for recruit training (required hours range from 70 to 240); 12 may set requirements for inservice training; minimum standards for supervisory and management training are authorized in only 2 states; none of the laws covers all types of training.

Other powers given to standards councils vary widely from state to state. Ten councils have the authority to conduct research. Some may approve training facilities and institutions; some may

63. U.S. President's Commission on Law Enforcement, *The Challenge of Crime in a Free Society*, p. 123.
64. Norman C. Kassoff, John M. Nickerson, and Kenneth Pillsbury, "The State of the Art," *Police Chief*, Vol. 35 (August 1968), pp. 75–78.

make studies and surveys; some may evaluate local agencies for compliance with the law. Minimum educational standards for entry into the police service can be set by 10 councils, mental standards by 9, psychological standards by 4, and moral or character standards by 14. Councils provide training programs and facilities in 12 states, in 4 cases at no cost to local agencies. In 8 states, councils reimburse departments for approved training conducted in other institutions. Because most standards legislation has been enacted since 1966, many of the councils are not yet fully staffed and financed to carry out all their authorized responsibilities. The training standards envisioned by the President's Commission on Law Enforcement may never be achieved as long as the goal remains voluntary for most local agencies. Left to the states, the adoption of comprehensive standards will surely be slow and erratic. Broader cooperation and some form of central direction are needed.

Federal Assistance

Establishment of standards at the federal level would in all likelihood be strongly opposed as contrary to the long-established principle of local control, but the issue has never been raised. Federal aid has been directed to more limited objectives.

Under the Law Enforcement Assistance Act of 1965, the $4.4 million spent to support police training included grants to establish standards and training commissions in 22 states, which laid a necessary foundation for future improvements on a statewide basis. Some four dozen other grants supported a variety of state and regional programs and projects, among them recruit training (individual awards), inservice training, and management training. There were no grants, however, for developing comprehensive training programs throughout the career structure. Several institutes were sponsored in special areas such as community relations and riot control and also some useful research on training needs and problems. But most of the grants involved a relatively small number of men: only 11 local agencies actually received funds directly to strengthen their own training.

Similarly, the Omnibus Crime Control and Safe Streets Act of 1968 authorized action grants for a variety of purposes:

1) Public protection, including the development, demonstration, evaluation, implementation, and purchase of methods, devices, facilities, and equipment designed to improve and strengthen law enforcement and reduce crime in public and private places.

2) The recruiting of law enforcement personnel and the training of personnel in law enforcement.

3) Public education relating to crime prevention and encouraging respect for law and order, including education programs in schools and programs to improve public understanding and cooperation with law enforcement agencies.

4) Construction of buildings or other physical facilities which would fulfill or implement the purposes of this section.

5) The organization, education, and training of special law enforcement units to combat organized crime, including the establishment and development of State organized crime prevention councils, the recruiting and training of special investigative and prosecuting personnel, and the development of systems for collecting, storing, and disseminating information relating to the control of organized crime.

6) The organization, education, and training of regular law enforcement officers, special law enforcement units, and law enforcement reserve units for the prevention, detection, and control of riots and other violent civil disorders, including the acquisition of riot control equipment.

7) The recruiting, organization, training, and education of community service officers to serve with and assist local and State law enforcement agencies in the discharge of their duties through such activities as recruiting; improvement of police-community relations and grievance resolution mechanisms; community patrol activities; encouragement of neighborhood participation in crime prevention and public safety efforts; and other activities designed to improve police capabilities, public safety and the objectives of this section. . . .[65]

65. P.L. 90–351.

Each of these purposes except the fourth concerns training, directly or indirectly. However, none of them provides explicit support for the development of comprehensive training for all personnel. On the contrary, grants for the specific purposes of the act are likely to fragment training further and make it more difficult to promote a comprehensive concept.

The priorities established in the 1968 act impose further obstacles. In allocating funds for action grants, the Law Enforcement Assistance Administration established by the act and the states must give special emphasis to projects dealing with the control of riots and organized crime. For fiscal 1969, three-fifths of appropriated action grant funds were mandated for these purposes and one-fifth was to be spent for the correctional system, which left the remaining fifth to be divided among training, equipment, facilities, public education, and the other stated purposes. Thus many departments may have sought funding for equipment or facilities; some departments may have conducted riot control exercises; others may have held courses in community relations or other specialized subjects. Some departments have been stimulated to improve their recruit training, or to inaugurate new types of inservice training, or to give greater attention to the training needs of administrators. On the other hand, some departments may have used funds under the act to finance more of the same poor-quality training they have conducted in the past. Of the $11 million expended for action grants in the first year of the law, it is impossible to identify how much—or how little—was actually devoted to the improvement of training.[66]

Expenditures for action grants in fiscal 1970 increased substantially to an estimated $98 million, and further increases are certain in future years. How much of these funds will be used to strengthen training cannot be estimated. A large share will likely

66. It is true that the act also authorized the FBI to expand its training activities for state and local law enforcement personnel and that $3 million was allotted for this purpose in fiscal 1969. Such expansion, however, may actually retard the improvement of those departments which are content to rely on the FBI for their training.

go to purchase equipment and weaponry, with undoubted benefits to the manufacturers but with questionable effect on the quality of law enforcement. (In fact, some officials are already concerned with the amounts of unneeded and shoddy equipment being purchased with federal funds by unsophisticated police agencies.)

At present, the only certainty about the effect of the law is that it does not begin to deal with the deficiencies of police manpower. It does not require any department to create a training system which meets the needs of all its personnel. The funds available for training will be of significant benefit to only a few departments, and will not be sufficient to bring about large-scale improvements in agencies throughout the country. No incentives are provided for departments to upgrade the content and quality of instruction, train more instructors, or promote higher standards of training. Only when such a comprehensive approach is implemented can citizens of every community be assured that the vital functions of preserving the peace and enforcing the laws will be carried out with reasonable competence.

CHAPTER SIX

A Crucial Decision for Law Enforcement

THE IMPACT OF the Omnibus Crime Control and Safe Streets Act of 1968, which authorized for the first time a substantial federal role in the improvement of local law enforcement, cannot fairly be assessed for several years: not until December 1968 were the first planning grants distributed to local agencies. From an early perspective, however, the act can be seen to contain some serious built-in obstacles to achievement of its primary objectives: "to assist state and local governments in reducing the incidence of crime," and "to increase the effectiveness, fairness, and coordination of law enforcement and criminal justice systems at all levels of government. . . ."[1]

Limitations of the Omnibus Bill

As a measure to reduce the incidence of crime and make the streets safer, it will probably have little effect. One scholar has already expressed doubt "that any of [its provisions] will lower the crime rate or increase the apprehending of criminals," since in his view the legislation places a mistaken emphasis on the police role in crime deterrence:

1. P.L. 90–351.

... It is by no means clear that the police are the most important agency for that responsibility. The police have the most visible and dramatic functions, but most police work is not concerned with catching criminals or even dealing with crime. The fraction of police activity that does deal with serious crime typically begins after the crime has been committed, and those criminals who are caught are turned over to other agencies (courts, prosecutors, correctional systems) for disposition.

In sum, an adequate response to the public concern over crime must begin with a recognition that we know relatively little about how to prevent crime; that, to the extent that it can be prevented, it can be only as a result of the operation of a complex criminal justice system and not just by more intensive police activity. . . .[2]

Thus, more effective law enforcement must be accompanied by speedier disposition of court cases, more relevant correctional programs, and increased citizen involvement in crime prevention. Since the act made no provision for improvement in these areas, it may be foredoomed to failure in terms of its first objective, which received the greatest congressional attention.

The act's second objective which was so little discussed—increasing "the effectiveness, fairness, and coordination of law enforcement"—has greater potential. Here, too, however, some grounds for skepticism have already been expressed. The requirement that states draw up comprehensive plans as a basis for making action grants requires them to assume responsibilities for coordination and supervision of police activities at the local level which few states have ever exercised:

... No one yet knows what a "state plan" for law enforcement should look like or what it might accomplish, and there is a desperate shortage of people who have the ability to create such plans, even assuming such creation to be possible.

One should proceed on the assumption that the state plans are not likely to be comprehensive sets of realistic goals toward which unified action can be directed. With proper guidance, however, they could assign priorities to the areas where intervention and experi-

2. James Q. Wilson, "Crime and Law Enforcement," in *Agenda for the Nation* (Brookings Institution, 1968), pp. 179–80.

ment might have the highest return in public safety based on current best guesses. But to accomplish even this, the federal government will have to abandon a passive role. It will have to develop clear, substantive guidelines, even model plans, disseminate present knowledge and the results of new experiments as aggressively as possible, and take an active part in helping produce program ideas.[3]

No matter how aggressive and creative the federal grant administrators may be, they will be limited by the act's special emphasis on the control of riots and organized crime. These misplaced priorities bear only superficially on manpower problems, which must be a central concern of any serious effort to improve law enforcement.

The act's failure to focus on manpower problems is most apparent in its provision for education and training. The President's Commission on Law Enforcement "emphasized many times the critical importance of improved education and training in making the agencies of justice fairer and more effective."[4] But the tuition grants and loans provided in the act will do little to elevate educational standards in the police service generally or to make good collegiate programs available to qualified students in every state. Nor will the limited grants for training projects bring about large-scale improvement in training at all levels of the police service— much less assure competent law enforcement in every community.

It may be that state planning agencies will encourage the development of comprehensive training systems which meet the needs of all personnel—if the planners show more willingness than Congress to confront police manpower problems. It may be that federal grant administrators will establish clear guidelines for evaluating the education and training that take place under the act. If these things occur, however, it will be more in spite of the legislation than because of it.

The National Institute of Law Enforcement and Criminal

3. *Ibid.*, p. 201. State administration of grants under the act has recently been criticized by the National League of Cities, which has charged that funds have been diverted from the cities where the crime problem is most acute. See *Washington Post*, Feb. 18, 1970.

4. U.S. President's Commission on Law Enforcement and Administration of Justice, *The Challenge of Crime in a Free Society* (Government Printing Office, 1967), p. 285.

Justice, established under the act to conduct vitally needed research, may develop more effective programs and methods for police education and training. But its studies will have little impact unless ways are found to apply the findings at the local level and to make the results known in training programs and college classrooms throughout the country.

The expansion of FBI training activities authorized by the act may create serious problems in the future. Despite its recognized competence, the federal agency cannot begin to do the entire job of training for all local departments or even a segment of them, although many may be prompted to rely on the FBI programs and defer needed improvements in their own training. Substantial increases in FBI personnel would be necessary, raising troublesome questions about the potential drain on good training officers in state and local agencies, the possible effect on the bureau's basic responsibilities in other important fields, the desirability of enlarging the national investigative agency, and the wisdom of giving it an inevitable measure of control over every local agency that becomes dependent on it for training.

There is another major handicap built into the act. The level of funding it provides falls far short of what will be required to have a national impact. Even if the full amounts authorized are appropriated, few departments will receive substantial assistance and the vast majority will benefit little, if at all. As has occurred in other federal grant programs, the agencies with the greatest sophistication in writing project applications may be expected to obtain the largest share of funds. Such favored agencies may thereby improve their equipment, facilities, and operations significantly, but such results could hardly be anticipated for more than a small fraction of the nation's police departments.

Because of the limited funds, one of the hopes underlying the act is that it will foster research and demonstration projects which may show other police agencies better ways to use their manpower. In all likelihood, however, the most promising approaches will turn out to require more and better manpower:

Suppose it could be shown that the rate of street crime in the highest crime areas of our large cities could be significantly reduced by doubling or tripling the number of beat patrolmen. . . . There is hardly a large city in the country that could afford (that is, could persuade local taxpayers to part with) the sums that such an effort would require for salaries alone. The new Law Enforcement Assistance Administration may develop and disseminate excellent ideas than no one can afford to buy. . . .[5]

These are critical limitations at a time when, in the public mind, the maintenance of law and order has come to require action and leadership at the highest levels of government. The conclusion seems justified that, however well administered, the Omnibus Crime Control and Safe Streets Act is an inadequate vehicle for achieving its stated goals.

A Proposed Program

If a systematic, long-range effort were designed specifically to confront the manpower deficiencies which the President's Commission on Law Enforcement identified as at the heart of the police problem, what would it look like? At the federal level it would focus on a series of related programs designed to stimulate and improve education and training for law enforcement. Following is an attempt to suggest its outlines and the order of magnitude of the costs involved in implementing such programs:

EDUCATION

1. *Establishment of curriculum standards*

   Support for a national board for accreditation of law enforcement degree programs $1 million

   From the examination of degree programs in Chapter 4, it is evident that the establishment of curriculum standards is of first priority. The need is urgent in view of the current rapid growth of law enforcement degree programs. The wide variation in the quality of these programs suggests that cooperation between

5. Wilson, "Crime and Law Enforcement," p. 200.

the educational community and the police profession on a national basis should be a necessary precondition for further federal support of police programs in the colleges and universities. The American Association of Junior Colleges guidelines, drawn up with the collaboration of the IACP and a committee of police chiefs and educators, provide a basis for development of more detailed criteria. (See p. 113.) The next step toward adoption of common standards and accreditation procedures might be the appointment of a national board, with representatives from each of the relevant professional organizations. Federal funds should be used to support its initial staffing and operation, under the provisions of the Omnibus Crime Control Act of 1968 authorizing grants for educational assistance. Such a board would provide a mechanism for continuing cooperation between the International Association of Chiefs of Police, the International Association of Police Professors, the National Sheriffs Association, the American Academy of Forensic Sciences, the American Bar Association, the American Council on Education, the American Association of Junior Colleges, the Association of Land Grant Colleges, and other appropriate bodies such as state educational agencies and commissions on law enforcement. The national board would promulgate standards, but actual evaluations of police degree programs would be carried out on a regional basis by special teams appointed by the participating associations and closely coordinated with existing bodies for accrediting educational institutions. Because standards will need constant reevaluation and because consultation will be needed to help individual institutions maintain and raise the standards of their police programs, the national board should be a continuing body, providing technical assistance and conducting curriculum research.

2. Strengthening the quality of instruction

Grants for the development of criminal justice centers at major universities $10 million

To serve as national models for quality baccalaureate and graduate programs, perhaps a dozen criminal justice centers should be established at existing major universities throughout the country. These centers would offer a broad variety of courses, taught by a faculty of outstanding scholars and practitioners in fields associated with the criminal justice system, including law, sociology, psychology, political science, and public administration. A few such centers of excellence engaged in teaching and research would quickly demonstrate the legitimacy of law enforcement as an academic discipline and attract a corps of able students and teachers into the field.

Predoctoral and postdoctoral faculty fellowships $2 million

To develop more qualified college instructors, predoctoral and postdoctoral fellowships should be provided for internships in police agencies, research in law enforcement education, and specialization in the law enforcement curriculum. In view of the shortage in this field, 250 fellowships a year would be a reasonable goal.

Visiting professorships for police officers $1 million

To encourage an appropriate mixture of practical experience and academic theory, qualified police officers should be encouraged to take leaves of absence of from six months to a year for full-time teaching. Federal grants could pay half the cost of the officers' salaries, with the academic institutions paying the other half. The program should be substantial enough to attract some 250 top- and second-echelon police executives as visiting professors each year.

Faculty institutes $0.5 million

To familiarize law enforcement faculty with new knowledge and techniques in the field, a series of short-term institutes for police professors should be sponsored in every region of the country.

3. *Encouragement of educational advancement for inservice personnel*

Educational salary supplements   *$2 million*

Another important priority is the development of incentives to educational advancement in all local agencies to counteract the attrition of qualified men from law enforcement to other fields. To encourage widespread use of salary increases for educational advancement, matching grants should be made to all agencies offering salary increments for two- and four-year degrees. A reasonable goal for inservice personnel would be 5,000 two-year degrees annually and 1,000 baccalaureate degrees, for which the federal contribution would be $250 for each associate degree and $500 for each baccalaureate.

Tuition grants   *$18 million*

Grants of up to $300 per semester to pay tuition and fees for part-time study leading to a degree in police science are currently provided under the 1968 Omnibus Crime Control Act. This program should be expanded to provide tuition grants at a level of about 30,000 a year.

Development grants to establish new programs   *$2.5 million*

Law enforcement degree programs are still unavailable to many of the nation's policemen. In those areas without programs, special one-time grants should be made to community colleges so that they can establish new programs meeting the accreditation standards of the national board.

Graduate fellowships for police executives   *$2.5 million*

Fellowships should be provided for police executives to undertake full-time graduate study in public administration or related fields. Full federal payment of the individual's salary would encourage local agencies to grant temporary leaves of absence.

Some 250–500 fellowships a year would be needed to make the awards available to a large number of departments.

4. Expanding opportunities for qualified students

College loan program for preservice students   *$15 million*

The current program of forgivable loans of up to $1,800 a year, with 25 percent cancelable each year of later police service, should be expanded to attract more qualified students in institutions throughout the country to a career in law enforcement. Up to 15,000 loans a year should be made available.

Institutional cost-of-education grants   *$15 million*

Institutions whose programs are certified as meeting the standards set by the national board should receive cost-of-education grants to help meet the instructional cost of each law enforcement student.

These proposals for new or enlarged federal funding would obviously impose large demands on the academic community. In Chapter 3 it was estimated that local police agencies would need at least 30,000 recruits a year for the next decade. If the needs of the state police and other governmental investigating agencies are added to this figure, the total comes to 40,000 a year. For collegiate programs in law enforcement to produce that many graduates annually would require an eightfold increase in the number of law enforcement degrees awarded, which would require in turn an eightfold increase in the number of students—to roughly 250,000—unless the present proportion of degrees to total program enrollment changes. If approximately half of the total number of students continue to be inservice students engaged in part-time study, the contribution to the upgrading of police personnel would be impressive.

The major burden of any large-scale increase would have to be borne by the two-year institutions, which enroll three-quarters of all law enforcement students. The community colleges are the logical short-range vehicle for extending educational opportunities. The Carnegie Commission on Higher Education estimates that 500 more community campuses should be established by 1976, for a total of about 1,500 such institutions, in order to make post–high school education generally available throughout the country.[6] This goal seems attainable in view of present growth rates, although of course it would be unrealistic to expect police programs to be established in all 1,500 institutions. Law enforcement programs have grown from 30 in 1960 to 199 in 1968, and enrollments have multiplied fourfold, but even if these trends were to continue at an accelerated rate, they would still fall far short of producing 250,000 enrollments. Clearly, police must make a major effort to recruit not only from law enforcement programs but from the general campus population as well.

At the same time these steps are taken, they should be undergirded by raising the criteria for entry and promotion in the police service, as recommended by the President's Commission on Law Enforcement. Federal grants should be used to strengthen and extend to all states legislation establishing mandatory standards for selection and training.

TRAINING

1. Establishment of training standards

Support for national training commission   *$5 million*

As in the field of education, top priority must be given to the upgrading of standards. A systematic effort to improve police training must begin with programs designed to raise standards of selection and training in all agencies and to rationalize police training as a continuing process from the recruit stage throughout the career structure. Because standards will not be meaningful

6. Carnegie Commission on Higher Education, *Quality and Equality: New Levels of Federal Responsibility for Higher Education* (McGraw-Hill, 1968), p. 37.

until they are established on a broad basis, a national training commission might be the means for obtaining reasonable uniformity among laws already on the books and developing cooperative proposals for strengthening them. The commission, which could be composed of delegates from state training councils, would be responsible for establishing minimum standards for training at all levels. Federal assistance for staffing and operation of such a commission could appropriately be provided without raising the specter of federal control.

Once established, the national commission would be an appropriate agency to exercise continuing leadership and direction toward higher standards of professionalization. For example, it could establish a national registry of all police candidates. Candidates could take a series of written, oral, and practical performance tests at local agencies or at designated places throughout the country for certification of their qualifications. Similar tests could be developed to certify the qualifications of inservice officers for promotion or for assignment as training instructors or other specialized duties. An individual so registered could then apply for a position at the level of his qualifications in any department and be assured that his credentials would be accepted. The national registry could also be used by state standards councils in making full-time appointments to state or regional academies.

Other functions of the commission might include sponsorship of special institutes on training problems, coordination and sponsorship of research in law enforcement training, technical assistance to the states, and promulgation of model curriculum patterns for recruit, inservice, and management training.

2. *Implementation of standards*

Support for additional personnel required to adopt training standards   *$60 million*

When the national training commission has reached agreement on minimum standards of selection and training, including recruit, inservice, and management training, federal grants should be made available to encourage their adoption. A direct and powerful incentive would be the establishment of a matching-grant program to meet the costs of the additional personnel needed to implement the training standards. In most departments, understaffing is one of the most serious obstacles to the upgrading of training, since more comprehensive training means more men off the street for longer periods of time. If police departments which accept the commission's minimum standards for all levels of training simultaneously received federal support to pay half the cost of a 5 percent increase in staff, the additional men would roughly compensate for the number of personnel involved in training at any time during the year. This would make it possible for agencies to improve their training and their effective strength at the same time.

Such federal assistance would differ significantly from general federal support of police salaries. General support is already advocated by some, but the proposal raises serious questions which are unlikely to be resolved in the near future. It would be a long step down the road toward a national police force, since it would make local departments directly dependent on the federal government for a substantial percentage of their operating budgets. The risks of federal control inherent in such a plan might be largely mitigated by the use of block grants for general law enforcement purposes. The plan is undesirable on other grounds, however: until significant improvements in recruiting and training standards have been achieved throughout the nation, the large expenditure of federal funds for general support of police salaries would not necessarily purchase any improvement in the quality of manpower. For the present, therefore, a more productive use of federal funds would be to underwrite half the cost of a 5 percent increase in personnel for all agencies willing to adopt improved training standards. This would effectively link upgrading with additional manpower. At the same time, it would not necessitate major federal involvement in the operation of local departments: grants could be made through the national commission upon certification of a department's training program.

Support for additional training instructors **$2 million**

Any national effort to upgrade training will require special programs to alleviate the shortage of qualified instructors. Grants should be made available to state and local agencies for up to half the salaries of additional full-time instructors hired to meet the commission's standards, provided they are fully qualified as training personnel.

3. *Improvement of instruction*

Regional training institutes **$15 million**

Under the general supervision of the commission, about a dozen institutes should be established to serve as model centers for advanced inservice and management training. These institutes could be established in existing facilities so long as one was provided for each of the several regions of the country.

4. *Provision of facilities*

Construction of training facilities **$25 million**

States which commit themselves to raising standards in all their local police agencies will have an immediate need for additional training facilities. Federal grants should be made available to pay half the cost of new training facilities constructed as part of a coordinated state plan.

The above proposals do not include any expansion of FBI training activities. It is assumed that the special courses at the National Academy, the regional institutes, and the schools conducted by visiting agents in local departments will be continued for the immediate future, since they fill a need which would not otherwise be met. The programs outlined above, however, would provide a more comprehensive approach to police training needs and would be preferable to further enlargement of the FBI role. As the proposed programs are implemented, as higher training standards are adopted and stronger state and regional programs are developed, the bureau's training activities should be modified accordingly.

The FBI has exerted pioneering leadership for three decades, and it continues to provide the only source of training for many departments. It should continue to play an influential part in law enforcement training, but its role should increasingly be limited to the demonstration of new methods and techniques and the provision of technical assistance upon request. Further expansion of its present training activities for police would inevitably give the bureau some degree of authority and control over local departments. The assumption of such powers by a federal agency would seriously undermine the principle of local control. It would also add substantially to the FBI's already extensive responsibilities. With the development of nationwide programs of federal assistance to local police agencies, the FBI should begin to concentrate its energies more exclusively on its unique and vital mission of combating organized crime and subversion, investigating federal and interstate crimes, and maintaining national facilities for criminal identification and information.

THE PROGRAMS suggested above, totaling slightly more than $176 million, do not provide a detailed blueprint; they only outline the dimensions of the job of carrying out the recommendations of the President's Commission on Law Enforcement for improving police education and training. The costs do not represent first-year expenditures but are approximations of annual spending levels that could be reached within a reasonably short period of time. Some of the expenditures would be nonrecurring; others would rise substantially as an increasing number of states begin to participate. They are rough estimates, but they provide an order of magnitude.

The cost of $176 million a year reveals the insignificance of current efforts. It compares with expenditures of $3.2 million for academic assistance in fiscal 1969 and an indeterminate amount (out of $11 million spent for all types of action grants) for training.[7] In the entire three years of the Law Enforcement Assistance Act (fiscal years 1966–68), *total* federal grants to police amounted to almost $13 million, of which $4.4 million went for training and $1.4 million for education.[8] The proposed programs are not intended to stand alone, but to complement other efforts such as those already initiated under the 1968 legislation. Grants for state and local planning, for equipment and facilities, and for technical research will continue to be needed. So will grants for innovative projects and for demonstration of new methods and techniques. Many projects in this category will be relevant to police manpower problems: for example, efforts to develop new approaches to recruitment (particularly among minority groups), the design of effective cadet or work experience programs, and the improvement of community relations. The manpower problems of the courts and the correctional system must also receive greatly increased attention.

Nor can any number of federal programs by themselves succeed in making law enforcement more effective. Major steps to modernize police systems must be taken at the state and local levels. The police service must give greater support to its own spokesmen for reform of personnel practices and administrative policies.

7. In fiscal 1970, $18.3 million was budgeted for academic assistance, and action grants were budgeted at $98 million (of which the amount spent for training was also indeterminate). The administration requested $24 million for academic assistance and $286 million for action grants in fiscal 1971.

8. Total federal support for police education and training during the three-year period would be closer to $9 million, including roughly $600,000 annually for the FBI's National Academy and field training programs plus incidental assistance from other federal departments. Under Title I of the Higher Education Act of 1965, college and university programs of community service have included a number of institutes, seminars, and academic degree programs for law enforcement personnel. A few local agencies have also benefited from other programs of the Department of Health, Education, and Welfare for research on the causes of crime and delinquency; from the Office of Economic Opportunity's support of community relations projects; and from the Department of Labor, which has made some manpower development grants to prepare young men from slum areas for police work.

Citizens of each community must become more involved. But whatever public and private efforts may be forthcoming, they should be based (as the President's Commission on Law Enforcement stressed) on substantial improvements in the education and training of police in every community in the nation.

If $176 million a year in federal funds is a reasonable estimate of the amount needed to improve police education and training, the President's Commission certainly underestimated the costs of a national strategy to combat crime. Reluctant to estimate the costs of its comprehensive recommendations, the commission offered only a vague estimate that "several hundred million dollars annually could be profitably spent over the next decade" for federal assistance for police, courts, and correctional system combined.[9] If it had spelled out the cost implications of its proposals, it could have impressed the public more strongly with the magnitude of the task.

A Crucial Decision

Although policies and programs to strengthen police manpower have not yet been adopted, a federal role in making local law enforcement more effective has been recognized as a necessity. This in itself represents a shift in popular opinion—one with implications of major social and political import in a land where law enforcement has always been viewed as a local matter. The 1968 presidential campaign demonstrated the popular demand for national leadership in the maintenance of law and order.

Like other political issues, "law and order" means many things to many people. To some the phrase is a coded promise to suppress dissent; to others it means protection of private property and individual rights. It may conjure up a war against organized crime, a crusade to make the streets safe, or a last stand for white

9. U.S. President's Commission on Law Enforcement and Administration of Justice, *The Challenge of Crime in a Free Society*, p. 284.

supremacy. Its very ambiguity gives the Nixon administration remarkably wide latitude in defining the issue and proposing solutions. No specific course of action has been mandated, only the necessity to act.

Not only the effectiveness of law enforcement but, ultimately, the quality of American life may be determined by the course of action chosen by the administration. Failure to develop adequate policies and programs to deal with police manpower problems will inevitably involve large social costs. These include not only the costs of crimes that competent law enforcement might have prevented but also the costs to freedom and dignity that result when wide variations in standards of police performance deprive citizens of their right to equal protection of the laws. Even greater costs may result if the police are not given the necessary support to keep the peace in a troubled land.

More effective law enforcement is thus a major imperative for the federal government. But the question remains whether policymakers will confront the evident deficiencies of police manpower.

REORDERING PRIORITIES

Less than a decade ago the public would not accept vigorous national leadership to improve law enforcement; today they demand it. Seizing the opportunity may prove difficult, however. Large-scale federal assistance for police education and training will inevitably require a reordering of priorities and an alteration of the traditional patterns of financing police protection. The costs will far exceed the authorized levels of the Omnibus Crime Control Act of 1968, and the benefits will not be immediately apparent.

Patterns of financing are determined basically by the ordering of resources. On the record, American society has failed to provide for the kind of law enforcement it requires. Other governmental services have received an increasingly larger share of local budgets in recent decades at the expense of police protection. Whereas 5.2 percent of local government expenditures went for protection in

1902, the percentage had dropped to a bare 4 percent by 1962.[10] If the effects of population growth, increases in motor vehicles, and increases in the cost per hour of police salaries are taken into account, there has been "no appreciable real increase in funds available to local police for crime control" from the beginning of the century.[11]

Failure to increase expenditures for the police has often been rationalized by the argument that increasing the share of the tax dollar spent for education, welfare, health, recreation, and related social services is more productive since these services will themselves reduce crime and social disorder and thereby the need for greater spending on police. But however attractive this view may be, it is specious.[12] Greater attention to social problems may reinforce social order in the long run, but in the short run it may produce further disorder as public expectations exceed the capacities of government. As for crime, much of it (particularly organized crime and white-collar crime) exists independently of questions of equal justice and better social conditions, as the President's Commission on Law Enforcement took pains to point out. This is not to deny the urgent necessity of the massive social action programs proposed by the National Advisory Commission on Civil Disorders "to fulfill our pledge of equality and to meet the fundamental needs of a democratic civilized society—domes-

10. Bureau of the Census, *Historical Statistics of the United States: Colonial Times to 1957* (Government Printing Office, 1960), p. 730, and *Historical Statistics . . . , Continuation to 1962 and Revisions*, p. 102.

11. David J. Bordua and Albert J. Reiss, Jr., "Law Enforcement," in *The Uses of Sociology*, ed. Paul F. Lazarsfeld, William H. Sewell, and Harold L. Wilensky (Basic Books, 1967), pp. 286–87. They note from their estimates that "there must have been a dramatic increase in police productivity as a consequence of the technological and managerial rationalization which has accompanied professionalization."

12. "Anyone here who believes that relief of poverty will bring a decrease in crime is in for some kind of disappointment," Lord Justice John Passmore Widgery of the Court of Appeals of England told the 1968 convention of the American Bar Association. The British believed this, he said, until they wiped out much of their poverty by welfare measures and eliminated most of their slums in the course of repairing the destruction of the Second World War, but crime has been rising in Britain as fast as in the United States (*New York Times*, Aug. 8, 1968).

tic peace, social justice, and urban centers that are citadels of the human spirit." [13] It is only to emphasize that they are additional to, and not a substitute for, the effective law enforcement required by a democratic civilized society. Political leaders must face the fact that present levels of expenditures for the police, courts, and correctional system must be increased significantly regardless of the urgency of other priorities. Since local and state jurisdictions acting in isolation do not have the resources to provide such increases, large-scale federal assistance will be needed.

A TIME FOR NEW INITIATIVES

The imperative for action poses a major challenge to the Nixon administration and a crucial decision for law enforcement. The most expedient course may be to seek larger appropriations and give high visibility to the federal role by accelerating the distribution of funds to a greater number of local agencies. This course, however appealing from a short-term standpoint, is likely to compound the more fundamental problems of the police service. The priorities expressed in the omnibus crime bill of 1968 reflect the traditional faith in equipment and technology as the means to affect crime statistics. The bill creates unrealistic expectations and accentuates many of the pressures which already limit police effectiveness. It may actually divert attention from the central problems of police personnel and encourage the tendencies of local departments to manipulate statistics, assign arrest quotas, buy more shiny patrol cars, and otherwise engage in image-building to justify further federal funds. As the public begins to realize that the additional expenditures are not purchasing safer streets or lower crime rates, the resulting disillusionment could deepen the alienation of the police from the rest of society and discredit any federal role in improving law enforcement.

On the other hand, federal initiatives to strengthen the quality

---

13. *Report of the National Advisory Commission on Civil Disorders* (Government Printing Office, 1968), p. 231. Chapter 17 contains its comprehensive recommendations in the field of employment, education, welfare, and housing.

and quantity of police manpower, as recommended by the President's Commission on Law Enforcement, could usher in a new era for law enforcement. It will not be easy to face up to the personnel deficiencies identified by the commission. But the time is at hand for the national administration to do so if it is to deal responsibly with the mounting public concern over law and order.

In one sense, the national concern reflects rising expectations rather than deteriorating performance. It is ironic that law and order should become the primary domestic issue at a time of growing affluence, unprecedented national efforts to alleviate poverty and other social ills, and increasing professionalization of the police. Just as law enforcement is beginning to make real progress toward higher standards, the public is coming to expect even better law enforcement.[14] With perceptive leadership, these trends can be made to reinforce each other.

In a more important sense, however, the national concern is an expression of the compelling need to heal the deep divisions threatening American society. Social unrest makes civil order not only vital but unachievable without the rule of law. More and more, social conditions are placing a premium on the competent performance of the law enforcement task. Rising expectations, population growth, and urbanization exert ever greater pressures on the embattled police agencies. One thing is certain: the pressures on the police can only increase in the years ahead. Continued erosion of the authority of the schools, the churches, the family, and other institutions of social control leaves the law enforcement agencies to deal alone with some of society's deepest problems. They are being delegated, by default, the authority to make important social decisions, but this delegation is not yet adequately understood or desired by citizens, public officials, or the police themselves.

The police, moreover, will not be able to perform effectively if

14. The paradox of American society entering the 1970s in turmoil largely because of its success is discussed by Kermit Gordon in his introduction to *Agenda for the Nation*, pp. 5–8.

a substantial segment of the population feels contemptuous of or threatened by them. If order and the rule of law are to prevail, society must assure that the authority and competence of the police both deserve and receive respect. National leadership could exert a powerful stimulus to this end. The administration could promote goals for law enforcement which go beyond technical proficiency in thief-catching. It could recognize the social responsibilities borne by the police and the high order of skills and intelligence needed to perform them. It could establish manpower policies to attract men with these qualities into law enforcement careers. As has been noted, programs to carry out such policies would entail major costs. What, then, would be the benefits?

They are many, though they are not susceptible to precise measurement. National policies and programs which encourage qualified young men to enter the police service, and assist them to obtain higher levels of education and training, should lay the basis for more competent performance of the law enforcement task in the streets of every city and town. Rising standards for the police service should foster greater respect and support for the police and broader understanding of their vital functions in democratic society. With understanding will come rising public demands that police meet the highest professional standards. Just as citizens are beginning to insist that the schools be staffed with qualified teachers for their children, they will insist that public officials provide competent, well-trained policemen to guard their streets. Government at all levels can then provide a fuller guarantee of the constitutional right to equal protection of the laws.

The current national concern for law and order, and the growing need for fairer and more effective law enforcement, could generate a comprehensive effort to upgrade police manpower, as the President's Commission on Law Enforcement urged. Knowledgeable observers have insisted for half a century that any such effort must be based on higher standards of police education and training. But whether the nation will respond to the need remains highly uncertain.

Index